THE
EIGHT-STEP
SWING

ALSO BY JIM McLEAN

Golf Digest's Book of Drills

The X-Factor Swing

Golf School

The Complete Idiot's Guide to Improving Your Short Game

The Eight-Step Swing (video)

Ben Hogan: The Golf Swing (video)

Sam Snead: A Swing for a Lifetime (video)

The X-Factor (video)

Visit Jim McLean at www.JimMcLean.com

TOM KITE'S SUPER SWING

STEP ONE: *The First Move*

STEP TWO: *Halfway Back*

STEP FIVE: *Move Down to the Ball*

STEP SIX: *Impact*

TOM KITE IS THE 1992 U.S. OPEN CHAMPION AND WAS THE ALL-TIME LEADING MONEY-WINNER ON THE PGA TOUR FOR TEN CONSECUTIVE YEARS.

STEP THREE: *Three-Quarter Backswing*

STEP FOUR: *Backswing Completed*

STEP SEVEN: *Early Follow-Through*

STEP EIGHT: *Finish*

THE EIGHT-STEP SWING

The Top-Selling Swing System That Has
Revolutionized the Teaching Industry

FOREWORD BY TOM KITE

JIM McLEAN

ILLUSTRATIONS BY DOM LUPO
PHOTOGRAPHS BY JEFF BLANTON

Quill

A HarperResource Book
An Imprint of HarperCollins *Publishers*

This book is dedicated to my family:
Justine, Matt, and Jon.
My wife, Justine, has supported my efforts
and stood by me as I traveled, studied,
and moved forward in my career as a golf instructor.
My boys, Matt and Jon, are the light of my life—
by far the greatest thing ever to happen to me.
I love you all.

HarperCollins books may be purchased for educational, business, or sales promotional use. For information, please write to: Special Markets Department, HarperCollins Publishers Inc., 10 East 53rd Street, New York, New York 10022.

A hardcover edition of this book was published in 1994 by HarperCollins Publishers
A paperback edition of this book was published in 1995 by HarperCollins Publishers

SECOND EDITION

Designed by William Ruoto
Illustrations copyright © 1994 by Dom Lupo
Photographs copyright © 1994 by Jeff Blanton and 2000 by Henebry

Library of Congress Cataloging-in-Publication Data

McLean, Jim.
    The eight-step swing: the top-selling swing system that has revolutionized the teaching industry / Jim McLean.—2nd ed.
        p.   cm.
    ISBN 0-06-095800-6
    1. Swing (Golf)   I. Title: 8-step swing.   II. Title.
GV979.S9 M32 2000
796.352'3—dc21   00-058187

        03   04   05   ❖/RRD   10   9   8   7   6

CONTENTS

FOREWORD

I cannot think of a more qualified person to be writing a book on advanced quality golf instruction than Jim McLean. In my opinion, Jim has earned the right to author this book. Why? Plain and simple, he has the knowledge. Jim has gone the extra mile to talk to the top players and teachers and pick their brains for any tidbit of information that may help him become first a better player and then a better teacher. Jackie Burke, Gary Player, Harvey Penick, Paul Runyan, Ben Hogan, Bob Charles, Ben Crenshaw, Don January, Byron Nelson, Ken Venturi, Claude Harmon, and even I, are only a few of those who have been quizzed by Jim.

But how one handles that knowledge has to be just as important. Jim has seen that there is not only one way to play the game. An experienced teacher knows he or she must take what the student has and work within those limitations. He has fundamentals that support his teaching. Fundamentals that are well supported by those players listed above. But he is not a "do it my way or else" kind of guy.

Jim has proven that with knowledge and versatility he can help students with a wide range of handicaps—everyone from the rank beginner to the veteran PGA Tour professional. This book will prove he also can help teachers improve their methods.

—*Tom Kite*

ACKNOWLEDGMENTS

At one time *The Eight-Step Swing* was a huge compilation of golf material covering the entire game. Dave Collins, one of my original Master Instructors, helped me compile a ton of notes and ideas I had put together over many years back in the 1980s. Dave put it all into a computer.

Two professional writers, David Gould and John Andrisani, then trimmed the book. David Gould first had the massive editing job of cleaning up a boatload of my ideas. Next my friend and former senior editor of *Golf* magazine reedited and reorganized the script and the artwork with Dom Lupo and the photographs with Jeff Blanton.

For the updated version, I personally gave a major effort to put the book together in a much more understandable way. There are now twenty-one chapters, nine more than the original. Plus I've added important drawings and photographs. Adam Harrell, the director of instruction at my Weston Academy, and Brian Bryson, my personal assistant this year, have greatly helped me in this effort. *As a result this highly technical book detailing the golf swing should be a much easier read.*

I have to give special thanks to Al Mengert, my first professional instructor. (My father, John McLean, a very good player, was my first teacher.) Al had worked under Tommy Armour at Boca Raton and Claude Harmon at Winged Foot. Jackie Burke is the finest short-game teacher I have ever known by a huge margin. You could ask his past students like Jack Nicklaus, Ben Crenshaw, Hal Sutton, Steve Elkington, or Phil Mickelson. Jackie has done numerous golf schools with me and has been one of my most important mentors for thirty years. Ken Venturi taught me more about shot making and the art of playing the game than anybody. We played probably one hundred rounds of golf together. Ken, a former U.S. Open Champion, learned his fundamentals from Byron Nelson and Ben Hogan. Enough said. Johnny Revolta was always a pleasure to watch and take lessons from. Nobody could teach a thirty-minute lesson better than Revolta. He was a teaching genius and not a bad player, winning many tour events and the PGA championship. Claude Harmon taught me his famous bunker shot repertoire. Most people believe he was the best ever in the bunkers. I've worked a lot with his sons Butch, Craig, Dick, and Billy. I've done many schools with Butch, Craig, and Dick. Gardner Dickinson, Ben Hogan's protégé and winner of eighteen tour events, helped me very much and gave me tremendous ideas. I loved playing with Gardner at Frenchman's Creek in Jupiter, Florida. Last but not least, I mention the teacher who has influenced me the most. He is the greatest researcher of the golf swing I have ever known and he is a great friend, Carl Welty.

Finally, I must acknowledge a few players, my college roommates at the University of Houston. John Mahaffey (a former PGA Champion), Bill Rogers (a former British Open Champion and ranked number one in the world in 1981), Bruce Lietzke (considered to be one of golf's greatest drivers and top tour player for over twenty-five years). Also at Houston during my time were Fuzzy Zoeller (a former U.S. Open Champion and Masters Champion), Keith Fergus, Jim Simons, Bruce Ashworth, Bobby Wadkins, and Tom Jenkins—all successful tour professionals. They all influenced my ideas on the game very much. Our college coach Dave Williams won sixteen NCAA Championships. I learned so much about coaching from him. When I left Houston we had won twelve out of the past sixteen NCAA Championships and finished second in the other four. What a tremendous person Dave Williams was!

All of these people have contributed to my understanding of the game and the golf swing. All of them gave me the most valuable gift—their time. I am greatly appreciative for the learning experience and the great time I spent with these supergifted individuals.

INTRODUCTION

I wrote and completed the original *The Eight-Step Swing* in 1989. It was submitted and then over a period of time was condensed into the book that finally came out early in 1994.

Since writing the original, eleven years have passed and much has happened. In 1994, I was awarded the National PGA Teacher of the Year Award. It was also in 1994 that I moved permanently to South Florida. From 1991 to 1993, I split my time between my summer job at Sleepy Hollow Country Club and the winter at my golf school with The Doral Golf Resort & Spa. I believe Sleepy Hollow may have been the best job in the Metropolitan Section. I had a seven-month contract at a beautiful twenty-seven-hole facility with a phenomenal membership and a PGA Senior Tour Event. We had three hundred golf members, skeet-shooting facilities, eighteen miles of horseback trails, stables that kept fifty horses, a great tennis program, and a large swimming facility. Also, I lived only four minutes from the club.

At Sleepy Hollow, we had a huge junior golf program for over one hundred children and our teaching program was second to none. At one time, we had three top–one hundred instructors in the world at one private club, plus two other superqualified teachers. Our membership included the Rockefellers, Bill Murray, Arthur Ashe, top people from Wall Street, and Jim Hand, a past president of the USGA.

It was Mr. Hand who hired me in 1988 when I held the dual head professional positions at Quaker Ridge Golf Club in Scarsdale, New York (site of the 1997 Walker Cup Matches), and Tamarisk Country Club in Palm Springs, California (site of the Bob Hope Classic).

Mr. Hand spearheaded the development of a (back-end) teaching range at Sleepy Hollow, which included my first real Superstation. Previously I used much smaller rooms to review swings indoors and hit into nets. This was a learning center built directly on my teaching side of the range to my specifications where you could step in and out directly onto the range (and it had three teaching stations). We could hit balls indoors out onto the range and review videotapes sitting down. Creating this learning atmosphere came from knowing Carl Welty and seeing firsthand the benefits of indoor instruction. Learning indoors is a key element to my teaching system and it is a mainstay at all of our golf schools to this day.

Sleepy Hollow was the Grand Central Station of instruction for all of the greater New York City area. It was common to have five teachers slamming lessons six days per week. We had all the top players in the Met area and it wasn't unusual to see Tom Kite, Brad Faxon, Mark McCumber, Jerry Pate, Peter Jacobsen, Gary Player, or some other tour professional hitting balls at Sleepy Hollow. Kenny Bakst took lessons there and won the U.S. Mid Amateur. George Zahringer was there at least once a week and he totally dominated tournament golf in the Met Section winning the Met Amateur six times and the Met Open plus every other major amateur event. Club pros like National Club Pro Champions Darrell Kestner and Mike Burke plus Bobby Heins and Bill Davis, among hundreds of others, came to Sleepy Hollow. We taught players who won every major junior, amateur, and senior event in the Met Section.

Besides this, I was playing more golf myself and was enjoying competing. George Zahringer and I won the National USF&G Skins game in Palm Springs, where I pocketed $61,000. My last year in the Met Section I finished in the top ten in all six events I played, including a runner-up finish in the section championship, the last event I played in the Met Section. In the Metropolitan Pro-Pro Championship playing with partner Kelly Moser, I shot a 27 for nine holes and a course-record 63 for the day. I had more good rounds those last few years than I had experienced since my college days. Working with one of my instructors, Dave Collins, I used my limited practice time (two jobs, two children, Little League baseball, etc.) very efficiently. In doing so, I definitely learned practice techniques that work great for people without a lot of time. All of what I used then for myself and now for my students is contained in the updated *The Eight-Step Swing*.

I knew moving to Miami would totally change my life. It would be a full-out commitment to teaching and I could virtually forget playing any competitive golf. Sure, I was already running Doral during the winter months, but this meant no more club professional life. It meant full-time schools, not part-time schools as I had done since 1985. Yet I knew this was the way to go, since teaching was the part of golf I loved the most. Without any question the decision to leave the club pro ranks was the best move of my professional life. The school at Doral Golf Resort & Spa has grown each and every year. In 1996, our golf school at Doral was rated by *US News & World Report* as the number one school in America. In 2000, an independent study by CNN also rated us number one. Best of all I know we have continued to improve each and every year.

Regarding my golf schools, I now have twenty-six PGA Professionals working at my Doral Golf School (during the winter months), seventeen PGA Professionals at my PGA West Golf School, five PGA Professionals at my La Quinta Golf School, and five PGA Professionals at my summer school site at Grand Traverse. I have a terrific academy at Mariners Point in San Francisco and another at Weston Hills in Fort Lauderdale, Florida. We are also the official golf school of the Asociacion de Golf del Valle de Mexico. All of them are extremely busy with teachers I have personally trained and we have had eight instructors rated by *Golf* magazine as among the top one hundred teachers in the world.

In 1995, I had been asked to join the fledgling Golf Channel as a Master Instruction Adviser. With a small start-up audience of less than 2 million viewers, I began my career as a TV instructor. Since that time, I have become a regular on the Golf Channel conducting my own TV show. As I write this, The Golf Channel now has over 30 million viewers.

Doral, where I spend most of my time, is one of the most unbelievable places on earth for golf. Not only do we have five really fine golf courses but we have a 700-room hotel and a forty-eight-room world-class spa. The Doral Blue Monster is our most famous course and it hosts the PGA Doral Ryder Open each year, where we usually get a tremendous field. All of the great ones come to the DRO and The Blue is certainly one of the best layouts the tour plays. In the summer of 1999 I was in charge of the bunker restoration (126 Bunkers) on the Blue. We also have Greg Norman's fabulous "Great White," which hosts the Shark Shoot-Out. Opened in February 2000, this golf course is one of the most beautiful and most difficult courses in America. The finals of the 1999 PGA Tour Qualifying were held on our Gold and Silver courses.

I hope you can visit us at one of our locations. I promise you will experience fantastic teaching. If there is one thing I have tried to do, it is to assemble the best staff and the best training of any instruction program in the world. I am sure you will notice it very quickly.

Most of all I hope you will enjoy this book. That includes my concern that you will learn new things about the golf swing and that they will help you progress as a player. I have rearranged the ideas from the original book and also presented the ideas more clearly with some significant updates. New chapters include a full listing of my "Death Moves." I also list the antifundamentals of golf, all of which you may want to avoid at all costs. When you recognize a death move in your swing, do not hesitate, change it! I also, possibly for the first time, actually list the fundamentals of the golf swing. This chapter, "The Fundamentals of Golf," gives you a concise list of items you can constantly work upon. There is a chapter on junior golf, where I give you my best advice on developing young children. A big part of our schools is dedicated to junior golf. Our program includes full-week junior elite training to simple one- and two-hour clinics we conduct. There is also a chapter strictly for women with an ABC approach and a chapter on the grip.

I also present a two-, four-, and six-step approach to learning the golf that we use in many of our schools. These are simplified ways to modify the eight-step approach. This chapter shows you different ways to use positioning. You will learn that there are numerous ways to use the eight steps to greatly improve your techniques and your ball-striking capability. The basic concept, however, is unchanged and it is a system for learning golf that I know works.

I wish you all the best of luck with your golf.

—*Jim McLean*

THE JIM McLEAN SYSTEM
An Overview of the Entire McLean Program, Including the 25 Percent Theory

Let me say straight out that I do teach a Jim McLean system at all of our schools. That means we have a certain way we teach the game of golf. I am very aware that most teachers refuse to admit they teach a system or they do not teach any system at all. I believe they are making a big mistake. For sure, a great majority of teachers are teaching one thing this year and then they will change it the next year. They may change even more often than that. To me, there are three basic types of teachers:

1. Pure method teacher
2. Semi method teacher (system)
3. No method (no system) teacher

The worst type of teacher for you is a (no system) no method teacher, because there is no consistency. Often a no system teacher is someone who has not taught very much, nor has a clear concept in his or her mind of what they are teaching. They probably teach what they are currently working on in their own game. This type of instructor will teach you something he read in a golf magazine or something that interested him on the Golf Channel. The biggest problem with this kind of teacher is you will work on something for a time and then come back and get a new way of playing or swinging from the same person. I have seen this type of instructor and they are certainly not people that I would want to work with myself. This very inefficient teacher is inconsistent and is someone most people will pick up doubt from. It is pretty easy to see this type of teacher does not really know what he is doing. On the other end of the spectrum is the pure method teacher, who has a strict set of rules and a precise picture of the golf swing. They teach the same basic lesson to everyone, and they get very good at it. Over time, that teacher can have a set answer for any question. There are several well-known teachers who are pure method teachers, but who say they are not, they definitely teach the same thing to everybody, at every level. You do not have to be a rocket scientist to figure this out. Just slightly different is the semimethod teacher. These teachers have a system that is more flexible. I created this category for myself so I could have my system fit into a category. That is, I have a strict way our instructors teach the game of golf, *but a very flexible way to use my system.* My strict way of training my instructors came from many years of observing the best teachers in the world, watching them teach many different types of players, and taking hundreds of lessons myself. There are several teachers who were extremely important to me, however, none more important than Carl Welty, whom I met back in Seattle thirty-five years ago. Carl has been a great friend ever since. I observed his indoor teaching method and was tremendously impressed with the progress of his students. I believe his study of the game is unmatched by anyone in the history of the game. I watched and worked with teachers like Jimmy Ballard, a great pure method teacher. He was very good for the more advanced player and he had a great system for teaching his ideas. Nobody was better organized than Jimmy and many modern teachers have stolen his material with no credit. He is the most criticized yet most misunderstood teacher I have ever known. Still, he was undeniably very successful. I then worked a great deal with Ken Venturi. What a phenomenal break that was for me. There are many things I have written down from him and I read them periodically to this day. One is, "if you take a lesson from me today, you will get the same lesson from me twenty years from now, because I am not changing; I also would have taught you the same lesson twenty years ago." He learned his ideas and fundamentals from Byron Nelson and Ben Hogan. Ken would say the lessons he received from Nelson and Hogan had already been proven on the battlefield. They also worked for Ken. I was tremendously privileged to work with Venturi and to learn many things from him. It was probably the most exciting thing that happened to my teaching and my long-game instruction has been hugely influenced by Ken. To work extremely hard with someone who was a U.S. Open Champion, play about one hundred rounds of golf with him, and watch him work with all types of students including Tom Watson, John Cook, and Tom Weiskopf was training you could never pay for. Knowing that Ken Venturi shared ideas he learned from two of the greatest players and greatest ball strikers in the history of the game of golf was very special. Ken would always tell me how crucial it would be to my career to teach the fundamentals of the game and to be very consistent. I also watched Johnny Revolta teach a lot in Palm Springs and took lessons from him myself and he had fantastic ideas. Both Venturi and Claude Harmon got many of their ideas from Revolta. Jackie Burke has been a mentor to me in both golf and other aspects of my life. Jackie helped me get every job I applied for and gave me tremendous ideas on the golf swing. I relied heavily on his advice on so many things. I worked with Harry Cooper at Westchester Country Club in Rye, New York. Claude Harmon worked for Harry Cooper in Chicago and always had the highest praise for his swing ideas. I also spent large amounts of time with Claude Harmon. I listened to him talk about all aspects of the game and I took several bunker lessons from Claude, who is fairly labeled as the best bunker game teacher in history. He had wonderful ideas on the game and he too had spent a lot of time with Ben Hogan. His son, Butch, now teaches those techniques to Tiger Woods. These to me were the most interesting teachers of the game and they got the best results.

I also started looking at other sports and tried to study the greatest coaches in basketball, football, baseball, and boxing. I watched Muhammad Ali train several times in Houston and I watched his fight against Buster Mathis in person. I watched how Angelo Dundee worked with him. To a lot of people my age, Muhammad Ali was a hero, and I enjoyed learning more about him and his other coach, Bundini Brown. I read about many other coaches, and I was able to get to know some of them personally. It soon became clear to me that the best coaches had a system that they taught and then they worked their players into that system. John Wooden had a certain way he had coached basketball, but it had to work with each of the new recruits that came in. Every three years he had a whole new basketball team, so he had to have a system that would work with all those different teams. When I grew up, UCLA basketball was huge on the West Coast. And being from Seattle, Washington, I went to many University of Washington games. I loved basketball as much as any sport and played a lot of basketball, including starting on a good high school team. So I was very interested in that aspect from a pretty early age. I convinced my high school basketball coach to use a number of presses and offenses I read about from John Wooden's UCLA Bruins. Later when I was able to have a six-hour meeting with Coach Wooden we talked a lot about basketball and his coaching ideas. I regularly call John Wooden and I seem to learn something every time from "The Wizard of Westwood." As we look at other sports coaches, for example Bill Parcells in football, he absolutely had a system of coaching the game, and a philosophy he totally believed. He had many different players work in that system, but he got a lot out of those players. People liked playing for Parcells even though he was a very tough coach. Why? He made them better and they knew it. Bruce Coslet, who was the head coach for the New York Jets and then later head coach for the Cincinnati Bengals, was one of the top offensive coordinators of the '80s. He also played under Paul Brown, who was one of the greatest NFL coaches of all time. I became very good friends with Bruce, and was able to go to the Jets' practices and looked at some of the notebooks he kept from his days with Paul Brown. I learned a lot from him and continued to visit Bruce often as he moved to the head coach position of the Cincinnati Bengals. During this time I often visited West Point, which I highlight in Chapter 18, "How to Prepare."

It was obvious to me that top coaches in all other sports used a system for teaching and coaching their respective games. It made sense to me that I needed my own system for teaching the game of golf. That took a long time for me to develop, because early on I was experimenting with so many different things. I started teaching full-time in 1975 at Westchester Country Club and I taught a tremendous amount there for five years. Each winter I traveled America to spend time with different top teachers. At Westchester, I was privileged to teach with Mary Lena Faulk, one of the people who wrote the introduction to *The Little Red Book* for Harvey Penick (the number one sports book of all time). She was very close to Harvey Penick and I learned a lot from her. She had a very simple but very effective teaching method. As I mentioned before, Harry Cooper also taught there. He is a Hall of Fame legend who won thirty-six tour events. Harry had an absolute system that he taught, which included specific positions. It was a style of teaching that worked particularly well for average people.

The turning point for me was in 1982 when I was asked to speak to fellow golf professionals. I was forced to articulate my ideas on the game of golf and how I taught them. It was at that time (1982) when I first spoke about the 25 Percent Theory to the Met Section Pros at the Metropolitan Education Forum in New York. There were about 300–400 professionals attending the forum and I worked very hard on that speech. It was scheduled over a two-hour period. I actually wrote everything out (the entire speech). A complete rookie move. The 25% Theory was something that I had given much thought to from playing the game professionally. It was my way to define the game and the separate components I needed to play the PGA Tour. I knew that

I had good physical skills but I had not played the PGA Tour full-time. Yes, I played in a few U.S. Opens and I played in the Masters one time. I competed on mini tours, Florida tour events, the Canadian Tour, and other professional events and a few PGA Tour events. My thought process was that there were actually several areas of the game to look at *that determine your total game.* At first, I did not know the importance of them, but I knew that there was more to golf than the long game and the short game. I added the mental game and then I added the management game. Upon closer inspection I gave them equal weight (each 25% of the total pie). *THE 25 PERCENT THEORY IS THE CENTERPIECE OF THE JIM MCLEAN SYSTEM. IT DIVIDES THE GAME EQUALLY INTO THOSE FOUR AREAS.*

From that first speech in New York, where I introduced this idea, teachers have agreed with me that golf is not just hitting the ball. The long game is the full shots and the golf swing itself, which this book will define in great detail. *The Eight-Step Swing* does not focus on the short game, mental game, or management game although I do write about them in the book. In fact I believe there are some excellent ideas on these subjects that may well benefit you, yet I have found from teaching the game for twenty-five years that the long game is the area people want to focus their attention. This is the most fun part of practicing golf. Going to the range, hitting golf balls, working on your golf swing, becoming a better ball striker, hitting the ball in the center of the clubface more often. That is what people enjoy most about golf. The all-out joy of a long solid hit. But still it is only one piece of the total game!

The second piece is the short game. Included in the short game is your wedge game: chipping, pitching, bunker shots, and putting. I figure it is from seventy-five yards in. Unquestionably this is the area where anyone going to our golf schools will lower their score the fastest. That is in part because the small pitching stroke contains the fundamental elements of your full swing. Most people certainly do not spend enough time on the short game. I do have arguments with other professionals about putting. Certainly it is a crucial aspect of the game, but I still put it in with the short game. I definitely do not believe it is 43% of the game. Because of how statistics can be manipulated, we can debate the true value of putting, yet certainly putting is a big part of golf. The better players I work with and who play in tournaments know that I focus huge amounts of time on putting. That too will be discussed here.

I wrote a book, *The Complete Idiot's Guide to Improving Your Short Game* (published in 2000), which is actually a very comprehensive short-game book and hopefully not really for idiots.

The third area is the mental game. I have seen numerous players on the range with beautiful golf swings. They were good chippers, pitched the ball well, and putted great, but when they got into a golf tournament they could not play. They could not make the toughest walk in golf, *the one from the range to the first tee.* The reason is they got too nervous, they froze, and they could not control their emotions. They just did not have it mentally to play the game. Other parts of the mental game are focus, concentration, and visualization techniques needed to play shots on the course. These are also tremendously important. In fact, if you ask a tour professional what the most important part of the game is, they would say the mental game. When you ask them the percentage they might say 80-90%. The only problem with that is the tour players are already great in the other areas. For this reason a tour player is not really the best person to ask.

The fourth area is the management game and I think we see management becoming more important. That is because it includes how you manage your life and your golf game. This area is comprehensive. When we look at who was the greatest manager of the game and their life it would probably be Jack Nicklaus. He would analyze the golf course better than anyone. He had a complete game plan. He always played smart shots. Jack also played to his strengths. If he had weaknesses, on certain days, he played away from them. He also had great visualization skills and wrote about this extensively. He had a special way of managing his time, before the season started. Jack would always travel to see his teacher, Jack Grout, in Florida before the year started and he began those sessions as if he was a beginner. That meant Mr. Grout took Nicklaus through every aspect of his golf swing and short game, from how tightly he gripped the club to how he placed his hands on this clubs. Mr. Grout would check to see how he started the club back, the full backswing, and the position at the top. Grout would work with him on his angles at setup to the position Jack finished his swing. We see now, on the PGA Tour, that Jack Nicklaus was way ahead of a lot of people. Very few people worked full-time with a teacher then, but now in 2000 we see just about every top tour player working full-time with a coach. Jack also kept his golf in perspective and kept a great family life that included raising five children. Managing also means getting yourself in good physical shape, your diet, and being totally prepared for a tournament. Many more serious golfers are paying attention to stretching and overall physical fitness. *The management part of the game focuses on your lifestyle,* and it is a huge part of being a successful player.

As I looked at myself as a player, I saw those four components. A tour player will be very good in at least three of those of those areas. I believe it is possible to compete on the PGA Tour and not be strong in one of my four components. However, you have to be very good in three areas. The greatest players on all tours are of course very good at all four areas. That is how I look at the game and how I analyze where I will start with each individual student during a lesson. When we look at most amateurs, the long game and the short game is usually the biggest piece we do as teacher. However, as a total teacher we also have to be a sports psychologist and we also should be able to show people how to stretch better, and how to get muscles in better shape. What I want to see at our schools are total game teachers. That is what I expect from my instructors. We work hard to hire the best instructors and then once I get them at Doral or PGA West we work very hard to train every one of our teachers on a continuous basis. We all must be on the same page to do top-quality schools. We are all talking the same language and we are all on the same system.

On this point when I first went to Sleepy Hollow Country Club in 1987, I began working with one of the football coaches at West Point and then had the opportunity to go to West Point Academy and see their Performance Enhancements Institute. That was really big for me in many ways. I got to speak with some of their coaches and trainers. One was the head coach of the football team, Coach Young. I saw some wonderful things at West Point, which was only forty-five minutes away from Sleepy Hollow. All of our facilities (including our Superstations) are designed in some fashion according to what I saw at West Point. You will read more about Coach Young in the chapter titled "How to Prepare."

THE SYSTEM—THREE LEVELS

In that 1982 speech I also talked about teaching at three different levels and again this is a huge part of what we teach at all of our schools. All of our instructors work at this every day. Those three levels are:

1. Beginner/Infrequent Golfer
2. Intermediates
3. Advanced (single digit to tour professional)

We teach the beginner and weekend player much different from the advanced player. I believe at level one you need to focus on ball contact training and educating the hands. So there is much more time spent on the hands and arms. That means lots of small swings and shots. The vast majority of golfers are in the intermediate category; I believe they need to learn some awareness of what the body does. I teach them body pivot moves and coordinating the arms and hands with the body. I also believe they need to learn an inside swing. To hit with power and from the inside you have to use some weight shift. There has to be a sequence from the top of the swing down to impact. To do this I teach another McLean fundamental. That is, golf is similar to other ball and stick sports. The sequence is similar. *It is a simple shift, rotate, and hit action.* This corresponds to other sports many people have played like tennis, baseball, racquetball, and also chopping down a tree. If you played these types of sports or could throw a rock far into a lake you have experienced the feel we are looking for in golf. That is not true with everyone; in fact, we have a lot of South American people who played soccer but of course did not use their hands and arms. I find it much more difficult to teach someone who has never played sports involving throwing or hitting. A lot of my teaching involves a natural athletic move. Notice I say *natural athletic.* *Natural* is a very bad word to use as a teacher, because natural is only what you do easily, it doesn't mean good, it means a habit, *but a natural "athletic" move means it corresponds to something that works in sports.* What works in golf is what works in any other stick and ball sport. This first means there is a loading action on the backswing, which can also be described as a move to the side, a coil, or a move behind the ball. Going forward there is a lateral shifting action from the back leg to the front leg and there also is a rotary motion of the body. If we're talking about a throwing action, it is basically the same move. You load or shift weight back, then you step toward your target, turn toward the target, and throw. That is the sequence we try to teach people. So obviously we teach a *two-pivot-point swing.* I do not believe you swing around a stationary post, your spine, or a single pivot point. *This is another key fundamental piece of the McLean system.* Learning the proper body sequence means you can more easily learn one of the most difficult things we have to teach in golf: to hit the ball straight, the clubhead must approach from inside the target line. A swing that starts forward with the lower body (or lower center) and not the upper body or the hands has a much greater chance to facilitate an inside attack track to the ball.

TWO BASICS

For the advanced player we move to the third level, and here we teach the big muscle action in much greater depth. You probably have heard of the "big muscle swing." I first clearly learned this concept from Venturi and soon thereafter from Jimmy Ballard. Advanced instruction means that your body center is initiating and the club is responding. The big muscles of the body are the shoulders, torso, and legs. They will dominate and lead. At all of our schools in our opening we use our time to separate the golf swing in *"two basic movements." What does the body do, and then what does the club do.* Another fundamental in the JMGS system is to immediately divide the golf swing into these two distinct parts. What you do with your body will definitely influence what the club does, and what you do with the club will absolutely influence what your body does. And according to each individual person that can vary. When I am on the tour or when tour players come to our facility, this is what most of them are devoting their time to. Another interesting point is that when I look at the body I look at two centers. I know most teachers do not look at this. I hear very few people talk about the two centers in the golf swing.

TWO CENTERS

Two additional components of my system:

1. Lower center, referred to as your true center of gravity, which is located at about the belt buckle just below your belly button. Also could be referred to as the body "core."
2. The upper center. The point at your sternum.

The two centers are not lined up exactly at address and they do not move the same way during the swing. As I look at what the body does in the golf swing, I look very closely at what you do with your two centers. At address, we find that the upper center starts slightly behind the lower center, which means your spine angle is tilted slightly away from the target (we'll discuss this more in reference to set and setup). These body angles become critical to the more advanced golfer. So the better players, once they train their hands and arms, no longer focus a great deal of attention on hand and arm actions. In fact, they try to eliminate or take out conscious manipulation with the hands. They are playing more with passive hands. Ben Hogan wrote eloquently about this in his book the *Five Lessons* and also in *Power Golf,* Jack Nicklaus wrote about it in *Golf My Way,* Jimmy Ballard said, "bad golf is played from the elbows down" and "the dog wags the tail." In the videotape I did, *Ben Hogan: The Golf Swing,* I talked extensively about Hogan's great descriptions of body sequencing. For sure the concept of body control is the more advanced explanation of what the top players are trying to do. The club and hands are more responsive, they are not initiating. The top player is not consciously hitting with the hands.

Now remember, in the earlier phases of golf it is critical to train the hands and we must do a lot of work in this area. As we get into the more advanced golf we are going to a more automatic style of playing. I often describe it as only a mild conscious thought of winding and unwinding of the body, with minimal use of the hands. When I do the opening presentations at my schools I look at my students and ask them this question, "What is your body doing in the golf swing?" I usually get a blank stare from all of them. This tells me most people have not thought of what they want their body to do in the swing. That is probably because so much teaching has been done with hands and arms. To me you must understand that the body movements are crucial in becoming being a better player. I always give a brief synopsis on body movements and I try to assure people of one simple golf truth: as you coil up (wind up) there are only a few things that go wrong. It is usually one of five or six moves that the average golfer makes improperly. I will be covering those Death Moves in both the back and forward swings.

THE TWO WRONG MOVES FROM THE TOP

There are two ways to go very wrong from the top, you either (1) throw the club with your hands and arms, or (2) unwind your upper torso prior to shifting. Either one of them is a Death Move. Simply, you are toast if you make either one of those mistakes.

DEATH MOVES

A Death Move, another mainstay of my system, is simply a move that any of my instructors is going to change right away. There are certain things I am not going to allow. I will have a chapter on the Death Moves, and as we go through each step, I will explain each possible Death Move that you must avoid. They are swing killers. (See Chapter 12.)

CORRIDORS OF SUCCESS

That leads me to another unique key piece of the McLean system, the Corridors of Success. I firmly believe that there are not exact positions in the golf swing. The eight-step system does not involve eight exact perfect positions. In fact, throughout the golf swing there are some wide areas for you to swing the golf club, which I refer to as corridors or parameters. This allows each of my instructors freedom to use their own imagination and ideas to improve students. If you look on the PGA Tour right now or go through the history of golf, anyone who has seriously studied videotape and the game of golf must come to the conclusion that there are many ways to swing the golf club. There are fewer ways to move your body, but surely where the club goes on the backswing has been highly overrated by many teachers with many methods and systems. In my mind, that has really hurt some young junior golfers, by taking away their natural gifts. Trying to have them swing the club up on someone's image of a plane line is usually a mistake (that plane line depends on where each instructor puts the camera and believe me, it could be anywhere). I want people to understand that there is no line going back, no perfect line, and whatever that line is, the downswing plane will be different. In addition, of course, it is the downswing plane that is critical. Taking the club away on a line is in no way going to make you a great ball striker. However, if you have a serious swing error and get out of the "corridor of success" on the backswing, we will change you. I do this because there are certain things you can do in your backswing that will definitely kill you. Remember, your backswing takes about four-fifths of a second and your downswing takes about one-fifth of a second. So you have quite a bit of time to place the club into a solid position or on the other hand to do some negative move on your backswing, while you then have *just a fraction of that time to fix it on the downswing*. If you roll the clubface open on the backswing in that four-fifths of a second time slot you now have only one-fifth of a second to square the clubface on the downswing. Things are happening a lot faster on the move forward. That is one reason that the backswing is important. A lot of amateurs (70–80% of the people that come to our schools) have either a poor grip or a poor move away from the golf ball where they open the clubface. They are dead in the water. From a poor start and then a bad position at the top they have to throw the golf club with the hands. Firing the hands from the top is the only way they can square it up at impact. So the backswing actually did kill them; it was the Death Move in the backswing that caused them to make a very poor move from the top. This leads me to the next part of our system.

TEACHING IN SEQUENCE

I teach golf in a sequence. By that I mean we use the building block approach. It is also called "first things first," something Jackie Burke beat into my psyche. Good teaching to me comes from teaching through a step-by-step approach, like a detective. I want to see what mistakes happened first. That mistake may cause a larger error later in the swing that may be much more obvious. Perhaps you lifted up through impact, or broke down coming in to impact, or you fell back on your right leg coming into the golf ball. These are almost always a result of a mistake you made earlier. My system involves looking at the swing in eight steps or eight positions or eight stages. All of my teachers are trained to check the swing in an orderly fashion. Now you can do the same. We are going to view the golf swing in total and hopefully you will look at your golf swing through these different positions to see what may be going wrong in your swing. By correcting things in a sequence, you have a chance to make a quantum leap in your golf game.

COPYCATS

Speaking extensively (around the world) on my system has caused me to deal with the fact that other teachers have exactly copied things that I have done at our schools, or copied my articles, or even tried to copy my entire system. One thing that helped me a lot was talking to John Wooden. Certainly people tried to copy his system at UCLA since he won ten NCAA Championships. Coach Wooden said that was okay with him, knowing that nobody could copy perfectly what he did. He also knew that there were other coaches who were very successful with different systems in teaching and coaching basketball. They were actually much more difficult to play against than somebody who tried to be exactly like UCLA. As I thought about what he said, I realized that it is just like something I tell all young talented players. Be yourself. Refine your game. When they watch great players, they might copy some aspect of their game. That is perfectly okay. However, one thing I have seen as a player and teacher is that when someone tries to copy another golfer's swing exactly, it never works. When you try to be somebody else, the copy is never as good as the original. I think that is a law of nature. We may want to copy the swing of Tiger Woods, Nick Faldo, Ben Hogan, Jack Nicklaus, or some other great player. However, it has been my experience that those trying to copy players exactly never realize the same success. Great players in fact are copied by other players, they are not copying someone else. *They are the real deal.*

I have seen things that I teach at our school, or things that I have spoken about written in magazines with no credit given. It has bothered me because I have definitely tried to give credit to everyone I talked to or worked with where I got my ideas. Also you have only so many original ideas in a lifetime, so it is natural to get a bit upset when someone else takes something and portrays it as if they came up with the concept or systematic approach. By crediting the people I have gotten the ideas from, I believe I actually enhance my system.

We all learn from others and I have used ideas from numerous people to develop my own unique brand of teaching the game. What we are actually trying to do at our golf schools is be unique in our teaching style. I am trying to be the Jim McLean

Golf Schools, trying absolutely not to copy other golf schools. *I want to be different.* For example, all our software systems for analyzing the swing are mine. Our system of teaching is trademarked, copyrighted, which I found does not make much difference because I know some people are going to copy it anyway. What I am assured of is that a copy is probably not going to be as good as what we are doing. There might be schools that surpass us with another system, but I know it will not be easy. Plus if they copy and do not give credit, eventually people find out. Besides, I do not think too many people are going to come near the commitments we make to be the number one golf school in the world. They just cannot copy everything.

I certainly know that it is much easier to say you want to be the best golf school than it is to do it. It has taken us years to be recognized as one of the best, if not the best, golf school in the world. We have been rated in several places as the top school and that does not surprise me, because I have been around the world and I have seen most other golf schools. I feel confident that we are doing a lot of things very well. I also know that there are other schools out there that are trying to be the best, and I expect that. I would be surprised if they were not trying to be number one. I do know that it takes a lot of things to go right and correctly to be considered a top golf school.

What you are reading in this book is what we have been teaching for many years. I know my system works and I am confident that the information you read in this book will help your game and will teach you a tremendous amount about how to dissect the golf swing, look at your own golf swing, make the corrections you need to make, and also when you need to make them. There is a section coming up called "Problems with Positions." You need to read this portion carefully because you cannot be out playing the game of golf thinking of exact positions, perfect positions, or going from this position to that position. You need to be a player and I will show you how to do that.

If you have a problem in your golf swing and you are not hitting the ball well, then you need to know what is going wrong and how you need to change that. Position teaching can do this for you. Use the eight steps to fix problems that are killing your game.

MAKING A CHANGE

To be an effective teacher I need to know *what that student is not doing correctly*, then together we both need to know what has to been done differently. From there, we need to know how to make the change. This is a very big part of the Jim McLean System. It is a three-step learning process that all of my instructors teach and talk about in every opening presentation. I am not exactly sure how I came up with it. I am not saying I am the first person who came up with it, because I think it is a pretty simple idea that can be used in any business. However, for golf this *"three-step system"* has served me well for many years.

THE THREE McLEAN RULES TO IMPROVEMENT

You as a player need to follow the Three McLean Rules to Improvement:

1. You must know *what you are doing right now*. That means not what you think you are doing, or what you hope you are doing, not what you were doing five years ago, or what you hope to do next year, but actually what is happening right now. That is why the video computer analysis we do is so important. You can do the same at your house or at the range with your video.

2. What should you be doing *instead* of what you are doing

right now? That means you have to have a clear picture of what needs to be happening as opposed to what you are doing.

3. Finally you must know *how* to make the change. That's where this book comes in or where a good teacher becomes important.

Most golfers go to their driving range in a very huge dilemma: they do not know what they are doing, plus they do not know what they should be doing. This leads them to listening to just about anybody walking up and down the range. That person walking up and down the range may be a 10 or 15 handicap golfer. What is he going to tell you? Probably he will tell you what he is working on with his swing, or what he read in a magazine, or what he saw on the Golf Channel, or some cliché to try to help you. This cliché unquestionably works for somebody at some time. However, the chances of that idea's being correct for you are very small. That is because what you are doing and what they are doing is most likely not the same thing. There are a lot of things that happen in a golf swing and it takes a pretty good eye to pick out what really is the cause of the problem.

"How to make the change" is the final step to improvement. This is where a top teacher, a top instructional video, or top instructional manual will lead you down the proper path. At our schools we say there are four basic ways to learn a new swing mechanic:

1. Read or be told what to do (verbal).
2. See or copy a model (visual).
3. Have a teacher move you into position. You "feel" the changes (kinesthetic).
4. A drill that focuses on the swing error and corrects the problem (drill).

THE THEORY OF ELIMINATION

A McLean Teaching Fundamental. The more an instructor can break down the movement of the body and the club into separate elements, the clearer the student's understanding of the Eight-Step Swing. Furthermore, through repetition of isolated movements, it's possible to accelerate the learning process.

Here are some simple ideas I have long preached on the general topic of "elimination and isolation for improvement." Follow this system in sequence, and you'll quickly break down any learning impairments that have previously blocked you from reaching your true golfing potential. It has worked well for me.

1. *Eliminate the Course.* Take away the course. Get away from playing golf on the course. Instead, go to the driving range and concentrate on swing tempo and swing position improvements (relative to the eight steps). Going to the range is a major stress reducer. Your golf muscles will be less tense, thereby enabling you to swing better.

2. *Eliminate the Range.* Take away the range. If you're not getting good results on the range, practice hitting balls into a driving net. This effectively eliminates ball flight anxiety. Without this deterrent, you will focus much more on the swing.

3. *Eliminate the Hit.* Take away the ball. In other words, focus solely on the swing. Now that the "hit impulse" is removed, you'll stop trying too hard and swinging too fast.

4. *Eliminate Bad Swings.* Take away the club. That leaves just the arms, legs, and body to do the swinging. Without the club, body awareness further improves.

5. *Eliminate Bad Motion.* Take away the arms. Fold your arms onto your chest and work on just footwork and body motion until you get it right.

TOP

All good players pay their dues at the range. This is the place to work on mechanics where you can hit ball after ball.

BOTTOM

Hitting into a net takes away the anxiety of where the ball goes. This can be very productive when making a change in your swing.

BOTTOM LEFT

By removing the ball, the golfer can often accelerate the learning process.

BOTTOM RIGHT

Making correct motions without a club enhances body awareness.

Most golfers look for most of their improvement through the long game. However, it is the entire package that makes a complete player. As a teacher and coach I try to touch on all facets of the game. As a player you need to look at all of the things that can help you achieve golf success.

I simply keep "eliminating" until the student makes improved movements and understands exactly what should be done. Once that is accomplished, we move on.

Many times a clear picture of the swing will allow you to eliminate any unnecessary actions in your technique. So, if you and your instructor can isolate any faulty movements and work together on a groove with only those choice steps that fall within the "corridors of success," you will soon evolve into a very efficient swinger. Once you accomplish that goal, you are on your way to being a true "player." You'll have a dependable swing that you can produce under pressure.

PROBLEMS WITH POSITIONS

Teaching the swing through steps or positions is not new, as I've already emphasized. My Eight Steps or checkpoint positions are different because of the parameters, or Corridors of Success, that I believe allow for necessary individualism.

Systems that tightly standardize the golf swing are dangerous because few golfers can perform all the movements and swing positions of the model. System teachers who use rigid guidelines close their minds and eyes to other swing actions and body movements that can and, in fact, do work.

Hitting "every" shot according to a rigid system for swinging the club makes playing under pressure tremendously more difficult. My own shortcomings in this area led me to understand that many things can be overdone, some of the oldest accepted axioms were incorrect, and some teaching adages such as "hit late" had to be reevaluated.

At an early stage of development, especially with youngsters, staying steady and delaying the hit can be taught very successfully. However, using the arms and hands to create lag is usually only a stage of development. At a later, advanced stage, remaining motionless, staying absolutely centered (the stationary post), and continuously working on lag not only can become dangerous but can promote Death Positions.

This one example shows that some positions, when practiced to an extreme, can cause tremendous damage even to highly skilled athletes and, in the end, make the game much harder indeed.

Position instruction, breaking the swing into component parts, or teaching through steps is a tremendous accelerator to the learning process. Teaching this way is especially good for isolating problems and correcting the fault. Yet positions have limitations.

When swing mechanics become the entire focal point of the teacher, the student ceases to become a skilled player. Instead, he or she becomes a confused, tense, robotic golfer.

When a certain position or set of positions become the goal, the act of swinging and being an athlete often get lost in the details. We need to remember that a true swinging action produces the consistency we all desire. I maintain that Corridors of Success allow individual differences and individual talent to exist within the Eight Steps. This freedom will allow extremely talented golfers to do it "their way."

Remember that wherever you learn golf, including from me, ideas or fundamentals are based on what we have seen, learned, or experienced. Science tells us that today's laws of physics may be proven wrong tomorrow. So there is no system that may not be improved down the road.

In my opinion and my experience, teaching through a series of steps has exceptional instructional value. Yet these steps, or positions, have limitations. To quote Harvey Penick, "Take some of the medicine, but don't swallow the whole bottle."

Finally, I always go back to my "25 Percent Theory." Practice the whole game. Remember it is not just swing. Realize we are playing the game of golf consisting of these four areas. Find out what part of the game you need to really work at. It may not be the long game.

THE 25 PERCENT THEORY

This is the cornerstone and centerpiece to all my teaching:

- The long game
- The short game
- The course management game
- The mental game

I know that for an advanced tournament player, the mental game is by far the most important element of the four. I know that hitting the golf ball is the most important aspect of golf for the beginner. We all know that improving the short game lowers our scores on the golf course and that some people build a strategy around their personal strengths and weaknesses much better than others. Often a less gifted player can shoot low scores by being mentally tough, mentally alert, and making no management mistakes.

THE LONG GAME

This encompasses your ball striking and the full swing. This is the area where most golfers spend most of their time and where they want to take instruction. They believe if they can build a perfect golf swing, they can play perfect golf. Nobody has ever done that, and even if you could, you still have three other areas of golf to master. The long game is critically important, of course, and also the most fun to work at, but I encourage you to look carefully at the other three parts of the game.

THE SHORT GAME

I define the short game area from 75 yards in for mid to high handicappers, and from 100 yards in for better players. This includes putting, chipping, pitching, bunker play, and getting up and down from trouble within range. Since the best players in the game don't hit even 75 percent of the greens in regulation, you can see how important the short game is. If it is possible for you, the golf course is a great place to practice your short game.

THE MANAGEMENT GAME

This is simply having the knowledge and discipline to manage yourself (your golf and your life). That means preparing yourself in every way possible in order to reach your goals. This might include a fitness program, better diet, and perhaps just slowing down getting to the golf course. It also means managing your game around the course, to avoid trouble and take the safe route, to avoid an unwise gamble. On the other hand, evaluating the circumstance of your match or the tournament may force you to take high risks, to focus on hitting the green rather than firing at dangerous hole locations, and to use a preshot routine effectively. In other words, the management game enables you to play golf intelligently rather than foolishly. See Chapters 18 and 19.

THE MENTAL GAME

This is how you handle the mental and emotional aspects of self, and determines your ability to take your range game to the golf course. Developing firm control of your mind and your emotions helps you play within yourself, frees your mind of extraneous thoughts and doubts, lets you concentrate on playing the game, and helps you perform more consistently to the level of your talent, especially in pressure situations.

Improvement in these last two areas might reduce scores more than any improvement you can make in the physical areas.

CLUB CONTROL

There Are Two Distinct Ways
to Move the Golf Club

When practice-range spectators gather behind tour players and watch them hit one long, accurate drive after another, someone in the gallery will usually utter the question: "How do they do that?" If they happen to be watching Justin Leonard, Jeff Sluman, Sergio Garcia, or some other player of lesser physical stature, they will probably ask: "Where does all that *power* come from?"

You can watch all day, but you will likely never really know where the golf swing's power, control, and leverage come from until you *feel it yourself.* A golf instructor's best moments occur when the students finally feel themselves swinging the club in a way that makes *full* use of their physical ability. Golf is as dissimilar as it can be from such clear-cut athletic acts as doing a bench press in weight-lifting. Unlike such starkly obvious functions, golf demands a complex series of movements to maximize the athlete's latent energy and apply it to the object to be moved.

In trying to take the invisible interconnections of the golf swing and make them visible to people, I sometimes use the following phrases: *the body hits the ball, the arms guide the club, and the hands fine-tune.*

Technically speaking, of course, the body cannot hit the ball, because the clubhead hits the ball, and the body is connected to the clubhead only via the arms and hands. While this fact may be obvious to a first-time spectator, the real workings of the golf swing are not. To me, there are two distinct ways in which the body becomes involved in the swing motion:

1. The hands and arms dominate and the body responds.
2. The hands, arms, and club respond to the body.

BACKSWING MOTIONS AND FEEL

OPTION 1: THE HANDS AND ARMS DOMINATE

This concept was made famous by the great Ernest Jones, who taught at an indoor studio in New York City. Jones was phenomenal and super successful with all levels of golfers. His teaching lesson book was always full and at a higher rate than any other teachers of his time. His book *Swing the Clubhead* is a true classic.

Players who employ this option start the club back with the hands and arms, and the large muscles of the upper body and the legs *follow* the club, or *give*, with the swing. The body is thus responding—immediately—to the swinging action created by the arms. This type of action is best illustrated in the swings of a first-rate female golfer or junior golfer. Their swings tend to be characterized by complete freedom of motion. Fred Couples and Meg Mallon are examples of professional golfers who exhibit this free-arm swing.

OPTION 2: THE HAND, ARMS, AND CLUB RESPOND TO THE BODY

This style is predominant in Ben Hogan's classic book *Five Lessons: The Modern Fundamentals of Golf,* which outlines brilliantly the basics of the big-muscle swing.

Here the hands and arms move as a result of motion originating in the torso, trunk, and legs. To be specific, the large muscles through the shoulders, sometimes helped by a push off the inside of the left leg or left instep, initiate the backswing and put the arms and hands in motion.

TOP
Fred Couples: the ultimate free-arm swinger

BOTTOM
Gary Player: a classic body swinger

As you can see, Option 2 is quite different from Option 1. In this second option, the body *center* dominates the takeaway. It serves as an inner engine to start the swing. Prime examples of contemporary players who employ this method are Jack Nicklaus, Greg Norman, Tiger Woods, Justin Leonard, David Duval, Nick Faldo, Gary Player, and Nick Price. In the past, Ben Hogan, Ken Venturi, Sam Snead, and Byron Nelson controlled their backswing with this one-piece take-away motion.

THE SEQUENCE OF LEARNING

In the hands-and-arms technique, the golfer feels the hands dominating the movements. This is by far the best way to learn the golf swing as a beginner. If he or she feels the body's involvement at all, it is perceived to play a supporting role. I believe it is correct for beginners and many intermediate golfers to "feel" the backswing in this manner. The reason is simple: we train ourselves in steps and stages. We crawl, walk, run, and then finally we race. *Golfers should feel and learn through their hands first.* You start by training your hands to move to specific locations or by copying the swing action of an accomplished player. *You learn to control and square the clubface with your hands.* Next, you train the arms to make a tension-free motion. Finally, you connect the hands, arms, and body motions into your swing center to become the best and most powerful player you can be.

THE ARMS GUIDE THE CLUB, THE HANDS FINE-TUNE

The second option for take-away and backswing, you'll remember, calls on the body, or the swing center, to initiate or begin the backswing motion and create a free-swinging action of the arms.

There is no thought or intent to guide the club into a position with the hands. The hands do virtually nothing. They go along for the ride. The feeling is they are "slung away with the big muscles in the upper body and shoulder." In Jimmy Ballard's oft-quoted words, "The dog is wagging the tail." I like to see the upper body and sometimes the left knee create a slight *lateral move* that puts the arms and club into motion. With grip pressure relatively light, the club is almost flung into the backswing, in a totally connected responsive action. It is the classic one-piece take-away motion.

This is the desired feeling for a seasoned player, even if he or she remains faintly conscious of the hands and arms keeping the club on its path. As you can see, we are training the hands for golf by consciously and gradually getting them to do less and less. Beginners learn to control the swing with their hands and arms, whereas experts come to have no conscious feeling of hand manipulation whatsoever for the standard bread-and-butter shot. Advanced players have trained their hands and arms. The workings of the hands are second nature and happen automatically, although for specific specialty shots the advanced golfer will adjust grip pressure and hand action (fine tuning). Ideally, the top player will feel the hands remain passive throughout the entire swing motion. He or she may feel the wrists hinge. But this absence of hand manipulation is a high-level skill that takes years to attain.

A POWERFUL, ACCURATE BACKSWING: THE VIEW FROM FORTY-FIVE DEGREES

Those spectators on the practice range would discern the power connections in the swing a little better if they stood facing the tour player but at an angle of about forty-five degrees off point-blank, toward the target. I particularly like this angle because there is a strong image of the upper body's full coil. It is especially noticeable in the windup of the left shoulder. The left shoulder muscles (the "lats" and "pecs") coil and appear to make a massive move back behind the golf ball. At the same time, the left leg appears to move—its movements look synchronized with the move of the left shoulder, but whether the leg initiates or responds is difficult to ascertain.

It is very clear that the actions of these two muscle groups are tightly coordinated. The forty-five-degree-angle view provides one of the best possible glimpses of the body's creation of energy to move the club on the backswing. The entire left side is seen winding the club up and behind the golfer. The clubshaft and clubhead, again, appear to be *slung* into the backswing. The relationship of the arms to the body has not changed from address; and we witness the *one-piece take-away*.

With the body creating the swinging action, this natural athletic move happens over and over; *it repeats easily.* Coming from the center and moving outward, the force can build and flow consistently. Therefore, the player builds a swing that can be trusted not to break down under the pressure of competition. Furthermore, with the body (rather than the hands and arms) initiating the motions, the golfer doesn't have to be concerned with specific perfect positions; that's because the triangle formed at address is maintained through the first stage of the swing. Of course, mastering that feel for the swing is not easy. If it were, everyone would be a great ball striker. Mastering feel takes time and practice. Only after a period of dedicated and proper practice does it seem to become clear and simple. In the end, it is the most efficient pressure-proof swing, and it is truly easier to repeat.

THE POSITION AT THE TOP

Moving on to the body's role in the downswing. I'm reminded of something Jackie Burke said more than twenty years ago: "Check the top five money winners each year. Look at their positions at the top of the backswing. Every year you will see five different positions."

Since that time, I have checked every year, and so far the statement has held true. The upshot is this: if there were a magic position at the top of the backswing that would guarantee all of us great golf shots, you can bet I would be swinging to that position and teaching all of my students to swing to that position, and so would every other instructor! But there is no one perfect at-the-top position. Getting to a certain position at the top will work for some players, but it absolutely does not spell success for all golfers. An exact location or position of the hands or clubshaft at the completion of the backswing is *not* a fundamental.

DOWNSWING MOTIONS AND FEEL

To reverse the direction of the club (from backswing to downswing), let's again compare the hands-and-arms-dominated motion with the body-dominated motion.

But before going any further, we will continue the previous point by stating this absolute: *It is the position of the clubface as the club starts down that is critical. At this point in the swing, the clubface cannot be extremely shut or be extremely open—in what I call a Death Position—where no recovery is possible.*

In an efficient downswing that is dominated by the hands and arms, the arms initiate a free swing down toward the ball, with the body responding. The feeling is of complete freedom and abandonment. The accomplished junior golfer is the classic example of this motion. Juniors usually have swings in which the loose, swooping action of the club pulls the body around to a full, upright follow-through. There is nothing wrong with this type of action, and I totally recommend it for a beginner and also for many average golfers who open up too quickly with the shoulders. The hips react to the hands. Many baseball coaches teach a hitting motion in the same way, especially if the batter is opening the body prematurely. This is a swing that will promote "draw" shots.

In a swing dominated by the body, opposite actions occur, yet the results can be far superior. Plus this is by far the best method under pressure. The force that reverses the swing's direction from back to forward comes first from the lower body or lower center (core) and is relayed immediately through the upper body. The last thing to change direction is the clubhead. To do this, there may be a feeling of the knees shifting laterally. The player may pump or kick off the right foot. There may be a feeling of the hips unwinding. Whatever the feel, the hands and arms are passive. They are put into motion by the weight transfer and rotation of the body. As a result, the arms, hands, and club lag behind, maintain width, and take almost a free ride into the delivery section of the swing. Everything is loaded and there is tremendous power in executing this move correctly.

A correct sequence of body motion allows the right elbow automatically to tuck into the right side. The club is definitely on an inside *attack track*, or slot, at the point we consider halfway from the top to impact. The weight shift forward and the right elbow tuck are tremendously valuable swing thoughts. These two movements happen in unison. Linking them together into a single motion connects the arms and body and delivers them into perfect hitting position. Harvey Penick is one teacher who had success with students, because he had them learn and groove these synchronized vital movements of the downswing, often in *slow motion*.

The only action required by the golfer from this point is to continue forward through the ball to a balanced finish, with 99 percent of the weight moving to the front foot. Centrifugal force, gravity, and an uninhibited free-swinging action square the club-head. There is no conscious manipulation of the club with the hands, as the turn of the body squares the clubface to the ball. This is the "no-hands" feeling top players describe. If there is a conscious thought by the top players, it is to have solid hands and *an absence of hand manipulation through the ball*.

The clubhead speed generated by this process is always a pleasant surprise to the average golfer, who tends to see clubhead speed as a product of consciously increased hand-and-arm-swinging speed. Actually it is the body that ignites the arms. Actually, maximum clubhead velocity is a by-product of *passive hands and arms.*

Part of trusting these physical facts is resisting the urge to throw or thrust the clubhead out at the ball through impact with your hands. As you'll soon realize through hard practice, the clubhead can get out to the ball simply by rotating your body center. There is no need to throw the hands out at the ball, although this is an incredibly strong impulse.

THE ARMS GUIDE THE CLUB

Because the arms are attached to the body at the shoulder joints and the hands/wrists are the connection between the arms and the club, it is the arms that should direct the path of the club throughout the swing. If the arms do nothing but stay in front of the player's chest throughout the swing, and if he or she has correct ball position and correct body motions, the club must swing on an inside-to-inside arc. *The shift action from the right foot to the left foot allows a long, flat spot and a longer on-line motion—still, of course, inside-to-inside.* Remember, golf is a two-sided game. Tension or conscious pulling of the front arm usually causes an open clubface at impact. It can be a real surprise killer.

SHOULDER ROTATION

To clarify further the role of the arms in directing the path of the club, it should be kept in mind that in a model swing the shoulders rotate at a ninety-degree angle to the spine angle. This is a very natural path for the shoulders to follow and introduces no artificial angles or club manipulation during the backswing or forward swing. The shoulders turn on an axis and there must be a smooth and constant rotation through to the finish, some-

The shift action creates an inside-to-inside elongated "flat" spot in the swing.

thing that cannot be taken for granted. This puts the clubshaft on a completely natural—and therefore repeatable—plane. The arms, then, respond to the motions of the body and move with the body. This keeps the arms in front of the body.

It is important to note that the right shoulder lowers because the lower body *initiates the forward movement*. The better player needs to avoid conscious efforts to lower the right shoulder too much by sliding the lower body laterally, because this action creates a swing plane that's too deep from the inside. (See Chapter 16, "Swing Left to Swing Right.")

Clubface control, by the hands, becomes far easier under the passive-arms, passive-hands approach. However, it does demand proper use of the body. By keeping the hands unified with constant grip pressure, you relegate the left hand and left wrist to a single responsibility: *not to break down! Inward bending of the left wrist before impact is probably the biggest power leak in the swing.* When the hands are in sync, there is no requirement for independent wrist action or for any conscious use of the hands to manipulate the clubface to produce your normal repeating ball flight.

It's my observation that the greatest players in history have particularly emphasized "no hands" when speaking about their swings. Does this mean they had no hand action? Of course it doesn't. To be great players, they had to have their hands working and releasing perfectly. *What it does mean is that they were not manipulating with their hands.* They did not have to consciously think about hand action. Their hands and wrists were trained and had no responsibility in the swing other than to hold on and go along for the ride. The feeling is that the hands maintain the address position throughout the swing. With great golfers, the hands respond automatically to the exquisite body motion.

THE HANDS FINE-TUNE

When it comes to specialty shots and purposely curved shots, of course, conscious hand action and variations in grip pressure do come into play. To hit a low slice or high hook, the player will use the hands differently than when he or she hits a standard shot. Partially through setup, partially through visualization, and partially through a conscious swing thought that includes wrist/hand action, the player will adjust to the special situation. The hands come into these special predicaments and *fine-tune* the swing action to produce various curving shots.

WHERE TIMING COMES IN

Under pressure of competition, a swing whose tempo and timing are controlled by the big muscles will be more reliable.

In looking at these four illustrations, note the changing role of shoulder-rotation during the swing.

Logic alone will tell you that trying to time the hands when the heat is on is a tough task. Many great players, particularly Ben Hogan, Jack Nicklaus, and Tiger Woods, have talked or written about the no-hands feeling. When it's time to fine-tune the swing to produce hooks, slices, high shots, and low shots, the hands are there to hold the club differently, to vary the grip pressure, to hold on through impact (block release), or otherwise to play a part. From Step Five in my Eight-Step Swing system, in the big-muscle swing it's as if the hands did nothing; a strong body turn is what enables the golfer to hammer the ball.

THE SET

The Universal Golf Fundamental

I often refer to the address routine as the set instead of the setup. I compare the golfer's need to go through a preshot routine, stand up to the ball, and then swing with a sprinter's need to take the mark, get set, and go. I don't look at the set as a separate item to be taught alone. I prefer to incorporate it into my instruction on the preshot routine. When players have gone through their preshot routine properly, they know the shot they want to hit and the ball flight they desire. But these decisions can be carried out only if the players get set to the ball in a manner that suits the shot.

Setup Basics. At address, you bend forward from the hip girdles with your knees flexed and "live tension" in your legs. Both feet are flat on the ground with the inside muscles of the legs and feet activated, and your weight is equally distributed on the entire foot, from the ball of each foot back to the heel. Usually, too, your hips are square to the target line, with the hip "girdles" pushed outward and the hip "pockets" four to eight inches outside your heels. The clubhead is normally in line with the hands, or within the allowable Corridor of Success.

Ideally, the butt of the club points between your navel and the crease of your slacks. Deviating from this configuration is not recommended. As long as you keep the hands and the club's handle between your body center and the crease of your slacks, you are within the acceptable parameters.

LEFT
Setup is not a step. Rather, it is positioning your body and club into a great golfer's address.

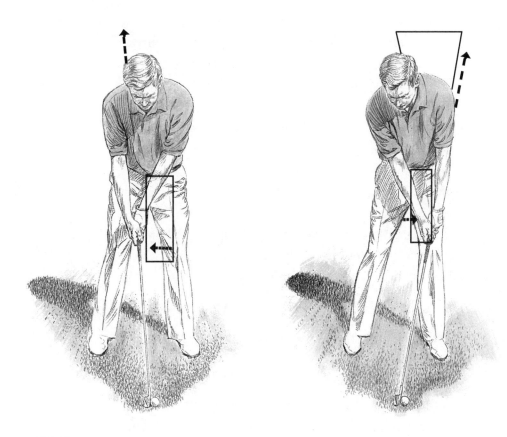

ABOVE

In setting up, be careful not to let your hands drift too to far behind (left), or too far ahead (right). The "Corridor of Success" is identified on this and subsequent photos.

SET YOUR BODY "PARALLEL LEFT"

An excellent starting point for the amateur golfer is to set up *parallel* to the ball-to-target line. I use the popular image of the railroad tracks to get this point across. The ball/target line is the outside rail, and the inside rail is the line the player uses to set the body alignments. This mental picture is widely used because it is virtually foolproof. Plus it presents a vividly clear mental picture that all students can easily relate to.

Along that inside rail, students should set their eyes, shoulders, hips, knees, forearms, and feet. Minor adjustments to this initial parallel model can be made with time. To simplify it, remember that the arms, which connect to the club, are attached to the shoulders. Therefore, the alignment of the shoulders is most critical of all. Because the right hand is further away from the body than the left, your shoulder line will be set slightly left of the inside rail. This is natural and also correct. Never set the shoulder line right of the hips. Rarely, if ever, will I set the shoulders closed. It is clear that the great ball hitters set the upper body parallel to the target line, or significantly more open, never closed. Interestingly, some of the great tour players whom I've studied closely set up closed with the lower body, open with the upper body—especially with the longer clubs.

ONE BALL POSITION FOR EVERY SHOT? NO WAY!

This is the obvious rebuttal to advocates of the "one-ball-position-for-every-shot" theory. To me, it is absolutely ludicrous to think you can play all shots from one position in your stance. Not only is most every shot you hit on the golf course from a different lie, often you have particular wind conditions and pin locations that require you to hit a low shot, high shot, draw, hook, fade, or slice. Instead of changing your entire swing and weight distribution for every shot, simply change the ball position. To hit different shots requires that you change something. To me, it is obvious that the easiest change is—*ball position*.

Let's have a reality check. To hit a short iron on a pure "tour-pro" trajectory—that is, relatively low with maximum backspin—will require a different striking action from a drive hit off a tee from flat ground. Of course, you could play that short iron off your left heel or instep, as one-ball-position advocates suggest. But then you'd also have to put 70 percent of your weight on your forward foot at address, set up with your hands well ahead of the

ABOVE

Ball position varies from shot to shot, depending upon endless variables.

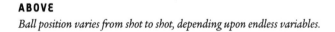

ball, increase your grip pressure, make a huge lateral move into the ball on the downswing, concentrate extra hard on keeping your hands way ahead of the clubhead in the hitting area, and drive the clubhead low through and well past the ball.

Wouldn't you rather just move the ball back in your stance and make a shorter, firmer version of your normal swing to hit this shot? Of course you would.

On paper, to a theorist, playing the ball from one position for all shots may seem like a good idea. To an accomplished player, it's a joke. Even if the rare tour player tells you that they play the ball from the same point in their stance on every shot, don't believe it. Typical pros have played golf almost their entire lives and, therefore, must be making automatic adjustments to different playing circumstances. If these adjustments are second nature to you as well, you can go right on thinking you play every shot from the same spot. Just don't start doing it.

Ball position moves from the center of your stance for wedges, up to the left heel for the driver. The width and positioning of stance make exact positioning off any part of the body impractical.

DISTANCE FROM THE BALL

Here I'm talking about the space between your hands and your body. As with much of golf, there is no perfect answer, but there are some excellent clues. For example, your hands are farther from your body with the driver than any other club. Teachers who say that the hands stay in one location for all clubs don't know what they are talking about. As each of your clubs increases in length and each lie angle is progressively flatter, the hands move farther from the body. Therefore the old adage that all clubs are a "hand's width" from the body is not correct. The other mistake I often hear is "you can't stand too close to the ball." I've seen golf's greatest drivers all with wide spacing between the hands and the body. However, with the short irons, these same players will have the hands much closer in. One easy way to establish the proper distance from the ball is at setup. Before placing the club on the ground, hold the club parallel to the ground and directly in front of your body. Relax your arms and measure the distance from the butt end of the club to your belt buckle. Then simply maintain this distance as you lower the club behind the ball. You'll be pleasantly surprised how easily this works.

ALIGNMENT TELLS THE TALE

Often, the harder you work on your swing, the tougher it is for you to believe that most golf shots are missed even before the swing begins. Be that as it may, a poor shot often is the result of poor alignment in the setup. Ken Venturi always drilled home the point that golfers don't lose their swing so much as they *lose their position at address*. "They don't get out of swing, they get out of position." The more I've taught, the more I agree.

Alignment is complicated by the fact that so many different body parts—the feet, knees, hips, shoulders, forearms, eyes—must be brought into position relative to the target line. Remember, the shoulders will actually be slightly more open. When you change just one of these factors, you exert some change on the desired ball flight. Pay attention to all alignments.

SET UP TENSION FREE

Tension is often a by-product of poor concentration, but in the golf swing, tension threatens to undo all your preparations. *Tension kills the golf swing.* A quick check for signs of tension is to observe the forearms, wrists, hands, and thighs. If the muscles are contracted and tensed, your swing is in trouble before it begins. Back away, breathe deeply and exhale very slowly, shake out the tension, then *reset* in a relaxed manner. Remember to evaluate your grip pressure on a scale of one (*superlight*) to ten (*supertight*), and for normal shots, keep it right around five or under (*moderate to light*). See pages 140–41 in Chapter 8, "The Grip."

THE SETUP POSITION DOES NOT SIMULATE IMPACT POSITION

I'm amazed at the number of students I teach who believe they strike the ball by returning their body to the same position they set at address. This is totally incorrect. To see the difference,

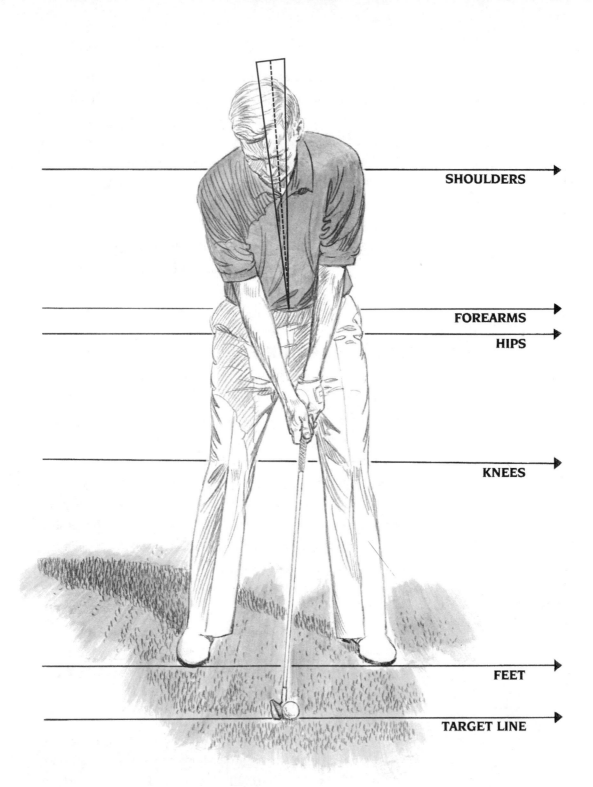

SHOULDERS

FOREARMS

HIPS

KNEES

FEET

TARGET LINE

LEFT

*Corridor of Success for Spine Tilt
(between 2 degrees and 10 degrees
of right side bending at address).*

RIGHT

*Address (left) and impact (right)
are not the same. In fact, everything
is different.*

thumb through some of your old golf magazines and view photographs of the pros at impact. The positions they are in do not
look much like their setup positions, do they? What has happened is that everything has shifted toward the target. The
weight is at least 70 percent to the left side. The hands are well
out in front of the address alignment. The left wrist is flat. The
right heel is off the ground and the right knee is kicking forward
at the ball. The hips are turned well left, at least thirty degrees in
a full swing. The shoulders should also be slightly open to the
target line, with the right shoulder lower and the left shoulder
higher. Clearly, not much resembles the alignments made during
the setup.

THE EIGHT-STEP SWING

Building Your Swing in an Organized Building Block Approach

PRELUDE TO EFFECTIVE INSTRUCTION

In the PGA of America teaching manual, they use the top five qualities of a top teacher from my education handout. Those include great knowledge, great communication, great enthusiasm, great motivator, and great presence. The first four are pretty obvious. The fifth, "presence," comes from being a successful teacher or player, someone who commands great respect so that the student going into a lesson is predisposed to listen, more than to a first-year teacher. Therefore, a teacher who has that quality has a huge edge on a rookie teacher. They will also have more success based simply on who they are, even if they are giving the same information. Those are basic qualities of great teaching and I will stand by them. However, I also want to talk about *what great teaching is not*. Great teaching is not having great clothes, although, at all our schools the teachers have beautiful coordinated outfits. That is not it. It is not having great range balls to hit; that is nice, but that's not it. It is not having a great facility; we have great facilities at Doral, PGA West, La Quinta, Grand Traverse, and our other academies. The setting is very helpful for teaching, but it does not make you a great teacher to have a great facility. It is a fact that many great facilities have very poor teaching programs. A great vocabulary certainly is not it. I have heard some teachers who are very smart and had a tremendous vocabulary. If you talk about the physics of the golf swing, they could explain the dynamics perfectly but they are still terrible teachers, so a great impressive vocabulary does not make you a great teacher either.

What does make you great is that the people you work with consistently get better. It is truly that simple. I have seen some teachers working at small ranges in very remote areas do unbelievable things. They may be teachers you have not heard of and who have not received recognition, but they are fantastic. I have seen teachers succeed tremendously without the great wonderful new high-tech equipment we have. However, I do believe this new technology helps us to be better teachers. By providing great equipment and facilities for my teachers, I know I give them a very big edge. Yet I have watched teachers without anything who give great lessons and really help people and really improve their games.

So, in reality, great teachers would be great wherever you dropped them on earth. They would be able to get the job done in any facility, and they would find a way to improve your game. I think great teachers probably have tremendous determination. To help a large number of people they must be very creative, and besides all of the main qualities I mentioned, they have another thirty or forty other important qualities. What I have seen is that the really great teachers are going to do whatever it takes to get the job done. By the way, that is the motto for our golf school, *"whatever it takes."* With some people, whatever it takes means giving a tremendous effort. It means really giving a lot of yourself and to me it means understanding total game instruction, understanding that the golf swing is one part of being a good teacher, while a great teacher has to look at all areas.

To me the 25 Percent Theory and teaching the four areas in detail is key. There is a lot of golf taught in all four of those areas. In helping people, many modern teachers are just swing mechanics. That is what they do. Some other teachers are short-game experts, and that is all they do. Then we have sports psychologists and they take care of that aspect of the game. A top teacher has to learn a lot about each area of the game. What I want our teachers to do is be total game teachers, complete teachers, who are capable of effectively teaching the whole game. Our teachers have to possess a broad depth of knowledge and an understanding of the many components that go into a golf swing. An effective swing, after all, is simply a swing that hits the ball solid and long with a certain pattern, with a slight fade, straight, or with slight draw, time after time and if necessary under pressure. If you don't think that is true then please explain funkier swings like those of Tom Lehman, David Duval, or Sergio Garcia, or Arnold Palmer, or Lee Trevino.

We have to look at what makes the swings produce great golf shots. What are the true fundamentals of golf? What made Bruce Lietzke the greatest driver on the tour for twenty-five years in a row, with a swing that went inside on the backswing, had the clubface closed at the top, and had a loop over the top? What made that work? And how many teachers would have, if they had the chance, changed Bruce Lietzke? That is a very scary thought.

PREPARING FOR THE EIGHT-STEP SWING

Before reading the next chapter on the Eight Steps, it's critical for you to know several truths about my teaching.

I don't teach the Eight-Step Swing all at once. Often, I do not even mention the steps in a particular order. Rather, as I analyze a swing, I mentally use these positions to organize my approach to each individual. It tremendously improves my ability to develop a game plan.

I then use these points in the swing to key in on problems. My teaching plan then becomes much easier for each individual lesson. My game plan is to diagnose the first problem in the player's swing. Once this is identified, I analyze why it is happening and then determine how I'll attack the problem.

The concept of swinging through eight steps is way too much for the average golfer. So when I use the steps, I simply eliminate three, four, or more positions. The key positions for the average player are Steps Two, Four, Six, and Eight. *These four steps should be clear in the golfer's mind.*

Many advanced players can easily adapt to all of the steps, if necessary. After an advanced player visualized the steps and then carefully swings through all of the positions, it's only a matter of time until it becomes routine. Soon enough, there will be no thoughts in his or her mind about swinging into or through exact positions.

In my system you need not attempt to master exact positions in golf. Nobody has a perfect swing. Trying to be perfect generally leads to overanalysis and a loss of freedom. Letting go, having freedom in your swing, is a huge key to golf success.

Placing the club through certain positions can, however, produce tremendous results. I believe that, to a significant degree, you can place the club into positions through the backswing. I sometimes have students think of the backswing as a "placement situation." If you know the locations, you can, in time, achieve dramatic results. The time required is different from player to player, but it can be achieved.

From technically correct backswing positioning (body plus club), the chances of achieving fundamental downswing and forward swing positions are greatly enhanced.

On the other hand, I believe that the move down to the ball (to impact) cannot be guided. Rather, you need to let go, to commit forward with abandonment. Think: *control back; let go forward!* Any top professional will tell you that to gain control of your shots you will need to give up control of your swing.

These eight steps are positions I have used in my teaching for many years. In fact, they are the same eight fundamental steps I used in writing *The Ten Fundamentals of the Modern Golf Swing* (videotape) in 1987. There were two pre-swing fundamentals and eight swing positions, four back and four forward.

STEP ONE: THE FIRST MOVE IN THE BACKSWING

The average golfer should closely watch the accomplished golfer make a smooth movement of the club away from the ball. Always strive for a smooth one-piece motion as you begin the take-away.

The point in the backswing when the clubhead has moved about three feet away from the ball may seem like a premature time for evaluation. Not so at all. This is *Step One* in a solid golf swing, and I regard this initial move as fundamental. In fact, if you can master the requirements of Step One, the remainder of the swing will fall into place more easily. If Step One is flawed, the golf swing is in a state of recovery until impact. It is extremely important to be precise at Step One. It is the one area of the swing in which there is little room for personal preference. Strive for precision at Step One.

BOTTOM
Step One: Two Views

THE MINI "MICRO" MOVE

What starts the club back? Interestingly, it should be a mini move forward. You can take control of this vital initial movement by triggering it with a mini move of your own choosing. I suggest you lift your right heel slightly and return that heel to the ground as a trigger. Or use a slight body press toward the target. (I don't teach the forward hand press, because it activates the hands too much in the take-away.) With practice, this ignition move becomes totally second nature and is usually unnoticeable to the average golfer. This mini move forward helps create a beautiful rebound or counter mini movement back to the right (weight shift). *Therefore, the first move in the backswing is slightly forward.*

The First Move Back. Then comes the first move back, which should be a *one-piece* action. In other words, everything together—shoulders, arms, and hands, and may include a slight shift with the hips and legs. Weight distribution in the feet can be sensed early—you are off the left foot and onto the right. The left-foot–right-knee action is critical to a proper one-piece take-away. Sensation in the feet should be slight, while the movement of the club should have an unforced, involuntary quality to it.

As the club first moves back, your head may move laterally or rotate a bit on any full swing. Although the head naturally moves, *both eyes* must remain on the ball. The head's slight lateral motion or turn accommodates a rotation of your upper spine and weight shift onto your right leg. *Many great ball strikers have early lateral head motion.*

Early on, the *axis* of the swing has shifted to the inside of your right leg. *The right leg becomes the backswing pivot point. The right leg is the post you will turn on.* Think of your take-away as a miniature movement to the side far more than as a rotation around the center of your body. Golfers who think "turn" as they go to Step One are highly prone to employing a "reverse pivot," that is, loading weight onto the left foot instead of the right foot.

The clubshaft, meanwhile, stays between the arms. There is no conscious effort to guide the club. The clubface stays square to the arc of the swing with usually no conscious rotation. Grip pressure in each hand stays constant (at a moderate lightness).

The job of the hands is only to *maintain feel*. The arms, hands, and club are put into motion by the shoulders and weight shift. There is a sensation that the club is swinging away freely, with no rigidity of the hands and arms. At the same time, control is maintained: you can feel exactly where the clubface is located and how it is oriented. In a natural swing action, which follows an arc, the clubhead rises up gradually along that arc. So be cautious not to overdo the dragging action of the club or to pick up the club abruptly with your hands. Top players may use descriptive phrases like "sling the club back" and "pump it back with your left knee" to get across the idea that the hands and arms are, to this point, only along for the ride.

A proper weight shift in Step One moves your weight to the inside of the right foot and toward the right heel. It is critical that you maintain the flex in your right knee during this step. The right leg is your brace. It accepts the weight transfer and helps maintain your hips at address levels.

If the big muscles of the body are used for the take-away, there will be no quick or jerky motions. Rather, the pace is even and smooth, setting the stage for good tempo with every shot. Many times the only swing thought a great player will have is "smooth take-away."

If you have correctly established the right leg as the backswing support post, you can pivot with a "connected" one-piece action. You will be off to a smooth start. It is a take-away you can practice and perfect. It is a take-away you can repeat under pressure and is the first key to consistency. Remember, it's not your job or your responsibility to pull the club inside the target line as a conscious act. This inside tracking will take care of itself, but if and only if your take-away is proper. Through the Step One position, the club will, in fact, appear and feel too far outside the arc of the swing. Unless you push your left arm out and away, however, you'll never be outside; just stay connected.

1. Freezing over the ball with no waggle and/or ignition before moving the club away from the ball.
2. Leaving the majority of your weight on your left leg, to such a degree that the left leg becomes the pivot point.
3. Overextending or disconnecting left arm.
4. Rolling your hands over dramatically in a clockwise direction.
5. Moving your head toward the target.

BASIC GUIDELINES

- Use some slight motion to ignite your take-away. A small forward press of the legs and/or waggle of the club should work well. I recommend a lifting and replanting of the right heel. Whichever trigger mechanism you choose, practice it and stick with it. Start your swing with momentum.
- Take the clubhead away from the ball smoothly in a one-piece motion (shoulders, arms, hands, and club start away together), making sure that your body stays level (does not dip or rise) and is free of any tension.
- When the clubhead is approximately three feet to the back of the ball, check to see if the clubshaft is still between your arms, weight has shifted onto the inside of your right leg, and that you have maintained the flex in the right knee.

MIRROR WORK

Practice at home in front of a mirror. Take the club away by choking down to the steel—the grip end will be in your stomach. This will demonstrate dramatically the "connection" in your take-away. Swing the club back and forth to feel the connection between your body and your hands and arms.

NEGATIVES YOU MUST AVOID

1. Raising your head or body
2. Dipping your head and body
3. A fast move away from the ball (usually with the hands)

Club in Center Drill

As you know from reading my ideas on Step One, this is a tremendously underrated area of the golf swing. I talk about this at every school opening I do. To illustrate, I start from (1) a bad setup, then (2) start the club away poorly, and with these two things going wrong you are history. Two Death Moves add up to no chance. The best drill to improve your take-away is the Spoke Drill; when you grip down on your club to the steel, the butt end of the grip would touch either your lower center or belt buckle area, or be just an inch away from it. The club is then easily seen between your arms and as the club starts away for the first two or three feet you maintain the original relationship. This is a basic one-piece take-away action, and the drill allows you to easily see when it is done incorrectly. You will see the club come out of center immediately. When done properly, as the club goes away, you keep the grip against your center during the initial move of the swing. Ingrain this move and you will be off to a great start. You can also do this drill near a wall, so you can see that the club will automatically work to the inside of the wall (or toward the golfer) during the take-away. It does not go straight back. The club will also start to elevate slightly: it does not drag on the ground. So the club works both in and up and it also works behind and around the golfer.

STEP TWO: HALFWAY BACK

Complete Instructions and Observation

We have reached the halfway back position when the club-shaft is parallel to the ground and the butt of the grip is pointed approximately at the target. This is an important checkpoint, although there is significant room for personal preference at this point. It's interesting to note that, at this split second, *the club-*

head is as far from the target as it will ever get. The clubface is square to the arc of the swing, with the toe of the "head" basically pointing upward. (Depending on the spine angle of the player during the setup, the clubface may appear slightly closed or downward—this is okay.)

At the Step Two position, when you're one-fourth of the way through the swing, nothing should be badly trailing or leading. The club, arms, and shoulders have stayed connected as a single unit. This is your backswing "package." At Step Two, everything has worked together.

Specifically, at this point you should have (1) shifted weight onto your right foot; (2) retained the same degree of flex in your right knee as you started with at address (there may be a little "float" with the right knee, but not much); (3) retained the flex in your left knee, broken inward and pointing behind the ball; (4) kept your right arm slightly above your left (in the manner of Lee Trevino) or well above your left (in the manner of Seve Ballesteros and Jack Nicklaus).

If the right arm is visible *under* the left arm, you have committed a Death Move, caused by either rolling your forearms and the club far too much to the inside of the ball-to-target line or leaving your body center still, in an all-arms take-away. In either case, you have swung your arms incorrectly away from your body.

It is important to note that the clubface position at Step Two is not tightly mandated. Nor are you required to have the clubshaft pointed directly at the target. Some of the top ball strikers in the world vary on these points noticeably. Bruce Lietzke, Ray Floyd, and John Daly, for example, take the clubshaft inside at Step Two. In contrast, Fred Couples, Lee Trevino, Jim Furyk, and Curtis Strange take the shaft outside at Step Two. All seven players, however, are able to correct and get back on plane during the downswing, which is the essential key to ball-striking success.

Slight deviations from the so-called perfect alignments and positions of the clubshaft and clubhead at Step Two are not to be tinkered with, if indeed you are able naturally and smoothly to self-correct them in the downswing. Our extensive studies at Doral indicate that about 30 percent of four players go above the shaft plane and 30 percent under the plane.

COMMON ERRORS AND POSSIBLE DEATH POSITIONS

1. *No hip turn and/or no weight shift.* This indicates that the legs were "dead" and the take-away was controlled too much with the arms.

2. *Locking of the right leg.* Overrotation of the hips or a reverse pivot accompanies this loss of knee flex.

3. *Rolling clubface open.* The clubface has fanned and rolled too far open. This is caused by overactive, independent wrist and arm action, very common in high handicap golfers.

4. *Clubface in an extremely shut position.* This error is the result of a manipulation of the club with your hands or an exceptionally steep shoulder turn. If you assume a weak left-hand grip or reverse pivot, you're likely to shut the clubface.

5. *Excessive extension of the left arm.* This error is most often caused by the player who pays too much attention to the adage "Keep your left arm straight." The long left arm is actually an overextension from the shoulder. It is indicative of an early disconnection in your backswing.

6. *Right arm folding immediately into the body.* The high handicapper makes a conscious effort to hold his or her right elbow against the body on the take-away. This is totally unnatural and it causes vital power to be lost with an excessively narrow backswing arc.

KEN VENTURI DRILL

This is the halfway back drill that I learned from Ken Venturi and is a drill I saw him use with great players and also average golfers. It is a drill where you take the club to Position Two (halfway back) and hold. From the hold position, you turn your body and then you lower the club to the ground. Ken would put a golf ball in second position opposite the back foot (middle of the back foot) the proper distance away with the correct amount of extension. You can do the same. Take your backswing, stop, turn, and take the club down. See if it was lined perfectly with the second golf ball, with no angles and virtually identical to your setup position.

LEFT
Step Three: Front

STEP THREE: THREE-QUARTER BACKSWING POSITION

Step Three is reached when the backswing is approximately three-quarters complete. It is an excellent position at which to stop and view your action on videotape. Here's what to look for:

- Your left arm should be nearly parallel to the ground and reasonably straight, but not stiff. It should also be very close to being parallel to the ball-target line. If it is skewed on an angle that takes it way off the line, you're in serious trouble. This is a clear-cut disconnection of the swing. The right arm has pulled too far around.

- Because the wrist cock is nearly complete, especially with your iron shots, the club and your left arm form an L. At this point in the swing *the club should feel light*. This is another place at which there is certainly room for personal preference. Some of the top players in the world cock their wrists quite early in the swing—such as Seve Ballesteros, Fuzzy Zoeller, and Nick Faldo. Others don't finish the wrist cock until later in their swings—for example, Greg Norman, Fred Couples, Davis Love, Tiger Woods, and Jack Nicklaus. However, at Step Three, most top players have cocked their wrists and formed the **L** angle when hitting an iron shot.

- You should have maintained the same "knuckle count" as you established at address. Your left wrist should not roll or twist, which would add knuckles. Nor should the club curl under, which would subtract knuckles. Either of these wrist actions can cause the clubface to close or open excessively off the plane of the swing. It's an idea I came up with to give students an easy check.

- In a model swing, the left wrist is nearly flat—in line with your left forearm. And the face of the club should be pointed in line with your left wrist. We call this a "square clubface" position. Nice to have, but not critical. Again, there is no one *perfect* position at the top.

- You should feel very balanced. *Note:* traveling from Step Three to the completion of the backswing is virtually a matter of momentum. A bit of wrist cock remains to be completed, but otherwise the impetus to return back to the ball is more or less dominant. From here we are set up just to carry on to the top, from which point the arms will free-fall back to the golf ball. We complete the arm swing and the full shoulder coil together.

- Grip pressure should be equal in both hands. On my scale of one to ten, grip pressure is five or less. Duplicating the pressure established during the setup is a good goal. Maintain what you had at address.

- You should feel that your weight has shifted toward the

right heel and slightly inside the right foot—but never toward the toes.

■ Your right knee should have retained its flex. The left knee, of course, is far easier to keep flexed. By Step Three, it has moved to its maximum extension.

 Right knee lockup tends to accompany weight onto the toes and also onto the outside of the right foot (a common but seldom noticed flaw). When golfers, particularly beginners, get stuck on this motion, they consign themselves to sloppiness in the leg action overall.

■ Your chin should have rotated to the right and/or your head should have shifted slightly. If the head remains completely stationary, the pivot becomes rigid and nonathletic. There must be a slight rotation or shift of the head to the right. Please understand, I am talking about the movement of the head. The gaze of the eyes should not shift or wander; it remains casually focused on the golf ball.

■ Ideally, you have not manipulated the clubface or your hands whatsoever through Step Three.

L DRILL ON PLANE

Take your 7 or 8 iron and place a tee in the vent hole of the grip. Now from address, take the club to the three-quarters position, and *check for three things*:

1. Most important, is the knuckle count on your left hand? Do you have the same knuckle count you had at address (if you do it means the clubface is square). If you see fewer knuckles you have closed the clubface. If you add on knuckles (which is very common), you have opened the clubface.

2. Is the tee pointed at the target line or slightly inside the target line? That is the corridor for that tee to be pointed.

TOP
Step Three: Two Views

However, we do not want the tee pointed to the outside of the target line (where the shaft starts to get horizontal to the ground), and we also do not want to see the opposite, where the tee would point to a line parallel to your feet. That would be too vertical.

3.   Does the arm and the shaft create an L position (close to a ninety-degree angle)? We use this drill to check swing plane, the position of your top hand, and also for the angle you set between your lead arm and the shaft of the golf club. It is a great drill to practice often and you can hit golf balls from here. By putting the club in the correct position, stopping, and then swinging at a ball that is teed up, you might be stunned at how well you can hit the ball in a very short period of time. Give yourself ten or fifteen minutes and you will be hitting beautiful golf shots.

STEP FOUR: 100 PERCENT OF YOUR SHOULDER TURN (BACKSWING COMPLETED)

Step Four is marked by the completion of the *back-around movement of the body and the club*, just before the return move toward the target. At Step Four, the upper body has completed its windup and coiling action and the uncoiling of the lower body is poised to lead the forward swing. Yet, because the lower body initiates the downswing before the upper body actually finishes turning back, there is no defined end to one phase and beginning of the next phase.

Obviously, flexibility, stature, and physique of individual golfers give different looks and lengths to the full backswing position. That is why I say to make your personal 100 percent turn on a full shot. For some that translates to one hundred degrees of shoulder turn, for others, seventy-five degrees. Therefore, there is no one at-the-top position to emulate. Having said that, certain basics for creating a sound backswing always apply. Let me now summarize those universal elements and body positions, relative to Step Four.

RIGHT
Step Four: Front

SUMMARY AND CHECKPOINTS

Hip/Shoulder Turn Positions. Throughout these step-by-step commentaries, the idea of connection is emphasized. All the same, at Step Four in the swing, the separation of the shoulders and hips is now complete. At this juncture in a full power swing, your shoulders have rotated eighty to one hundred twenty degrees and your hips have turned between forty and sixty-five degrees. This is just a model for simple numbers. Your left shoulder is behind the ball and close to being in line with the inside of your right leg. Of course, partial shots like a punched 8 iron would follow a miniature version of this. For a general picture, the shoulders turn twice as much as the hips on most shots. A huge key is to think of the backswing as a major coil behind the ball. That image, which I wrote about extensively in *The X Factor,* seems to create the best image for most golfers.

Knee Action. Your left knee is pointed slightly behind the ball but is stable. Your left heel may be slightly off the ground for longer shots. Most tour players keep the left heel down, but it is okay for the heel to come off the ground if it is "pulled" off as a result of a proper pivot. Under no condition should it be consciously lifted. Meanwhile, your right knee has retained flex and is stable. You shouldn't lose the flex in your right knee, or you'll give up all the good body lines you established at address. Your knees have turned approximately twenty-five degrees (see figure at right on page 72). Place a clubshaft across your knees at the completion of the backswing to check. At the top of the backswing, the lower body has already just started back to the left. The knee turn is approximately 25 percent of the total shoulder turn and 50 percent of the hip turn.

Weight Shift. Your weight should be toward the right heel and on top of the right foot. This is very important. If the weight goes to the outside of your right foot or toward the toes, balance is impaired. RHP stands for right hip pocket back, a phrase used by Greg Norman. It's a great thought that works wonders for many golfers making a faulty coil.

Footwork. Good footwork in the backswing is critical to good shot making. Therefore, you want to roll weight off the inside of your left foot. Ankle flexibility is needed for this rolling—practice it often. Also, connection of the left heel with the ground is important. On most shots, the left heel doesn't leave the ground. On longer shots, it should not rise more than an inch or so. Last, your footwork should be rhythmic. Thinking of the golf swing as a *dance step* will help you accomplish that goal.

Head and Chin Positions. Your chin must rotate its maximum distance to the right by Step Four. In some players, this may be as much as forty-five degrees. The average rotation is twenty to twenty-five degrees. In addition, close scrutiny of hundreds of great players' swings on stop-action video shows there may be a lateral shift of the head of between one and four inches, or more. None of the great players freezes the head in the address position.

Left Arm Position. Your left arm may be slightly bent at the elbow. The key point is that it be firm but not stiff, rigid, and full of tension. Golfers have read and heard so much about a straight left arm, they tend consciously to stiffen it in an effort to avoid any bend. In fact, our studies at Doral testing every player competing in the Doral Ryder Open (for nine years) indicates that approximately 95 percent of all tour players have left arm bend.

Left Arm Angle. A critical observation is the angle of the left arm at Step Four. The ideal angle would closely match the angle of the shaft (whichever club is being hit).

Hand Action. Once you've completed your pivot, keep your hands *quiet*. Many players, hoping to gain distance by increasing the size of their swing arc, will continue to swing their arms and hands upward after the pivot is complete. In fact, this attempt to pick up clubhead speed and add power to the swing almost always backfires. Overswinging the hands causes disconnection between the swing center and the club. The clubshaft gets thrown above the plane and, on the downswing, will usually cross over the ball-to-target line. This impairs flush impact and sets up the slice or any variety of weak shots. An excellent check is: the point of your left hip, your shoulders, and your arms all arrive at Step Four together. Remember to practice the feel of the hands, arms, and shoulders arriving at the top together.

Wrist Position.   There is no precisely perfect wrist position at the top of the swing, no position that will guarantee a return of the clubhead to the ball in a completely square angle. Hand size, grip configuration, strength, and the degree of lateral motion during the downswing all influence clubface angle. Among top players, Tom Watson, John Mahaffey, Lee Trevino, Tom Weiskopf, and Bruce Lietzke tend to exhibit closed clubface angles at the top, while Ben Hogan, Curtis Strange, José María Olazabal, and Johnny Miller, to name a few, have had the clubface open at the top.

Parameters of preference are allowed in clubface orientation at the top. I'm concerned only when the parameters are exceeded and the student exhibits a supershut or superopen clubface at Step Four or when the student cannot square the clubface from his or her present top-of-the-swing position. This said, I personally prefer square or slightly closed. Most amateurs have the face open.

Shoulder/Arm Relationship.   The arms swing in front of your body center. Even though momentum will carry the arms somewhat up and across the chest, a good swing thought is, "When the shoulders stop winding the arms, stop swinging."

1.   Even if you had yourself in good positions through Steps One, Two, and Three, you are at risk of tipping your body weight back to your left side, if you overturn your shoulders and arms at Step Four. That "little extra" you strive for at Step Four can lead to a legitimate Death Move. It is possible to overturn.

2.   In a model natural swing, the clubface will always appear open in the backswing, then closed again past impact. Step Four should find it in a position that allows you to "get to impact square." If the clubface is turned drastically skyward (extremely closed) at this point in the swing, trouble awaits you. This position is almost impossible to recover from.

3. If you are wide open at the top, you'll tend to throw your hands at the ball through impact and hit a slice shot right of target. The wide-open position is very common to the high handicap player. So use video to check your clubface at-the-top position.

SPLIT GRIP FULL BACK SWING

From address, we split our hands several inches apart. As you go back, it will be very apparent to you if you make any rolls or twists of the golf club. As you swing the club back to the top, you will sense how the hands and the two arms work together to get the club back and pointed down the target line at the top of the backswing. As you do this, you want to synchronize your body coil and arm swing, and again, with a split grip it is very easy to sense and feel. You will definitely feel if you close the clubface and twist the club down with your right palm under at the top. You will also easily feel if the left wrist crimps inward and puts the club in an open position, an extremely common Death Move error. This drill will give you the correct feel.

BODY DRILL

Point your left forefinger in the center of your chest, your elbow pointed at the target. From a good setup, coil behind the golf ball. This is a staple in our schools and I call this the McLean coil drill because it is one of only a few that I truly invented. I use this drill to have my students feel upper center and train students to feel and see how much upper center moves. It also becomes very apparent how far the left elbow moves when you do this. Notice where you are at address and then where you are at the top of the backswing, and you can see how far back center moved. This body drill is done mostly with the upper body. Put your right hand out in front of your chest at address. Then notice where you get your right arm at the top. You get a good right arm position mostly through body coil. At the top of the backswing, make sure your weight is balanced in the middle of your back foot. Keep some flexion in the back knee and understand your weight is toward the back heel. Do not let your right knee straighten out and you will be in pretty good shape. Make sure you get the upper center over the inside part of your back leg. *Also you must remain level,* do not lift up out of your posture and do not drop down or dip as you practice this drill.

STEP FIVE: MOVE DOWN TO THE BALL

If there is a secret to employing a good golf swing, it occurs here.

In all of the great swings I have studied, there is no evidence of a "stop" and "start" that together reverse the direction of the club from backswing to downswing. Instead, I see a smooth, flowing transition. The arms, hands, and club respond to the actions of the lower body or lower center of body. In fine golf swings, the last thing to change direction at the top is the clubhead. This, of course, makes perfect sense, because all the centrifugal and centripetal force we apply in the swing is designed to do nothing else but load the clubhead with energy and deliver it down the proper path.

In the transition, your arms and hands are passive. The first move is backward and down. The clubhead sinks lower as your hips start to unwind. Your hands and wrists respond immediately to the reversal of direction. Your right elbow automatically

TOP
Step Five: Front

BOTTOM
The move down to Step Five

drops into the proper slot by your right side. The Step Five checkpoint position in many ways resembles the Step Three position on the backswing. From a head-on view, it looks as if the hands and clubshaft were passing back through the same positions they were in at Step Three (*only considerably narrower*). There is a sense that the hands free-fall down to the delivery position.

The right shoulder helps determine the path of the downswing. If, in its first motion, your right shoulder rocks down, all systems are go. Thanks to the shoulder, your right elbow can now drop into its proper slot and align (head-on view) with your right hip. This lowering of the right shoulder is a response to the legs' initiating the forward motion. But if the first motion is initiated by your right shoulder out toward the ball, you've got no chance to attain the correct positions at Step Five. This down tuck of the right shoulder can be overworked, so proceed with caution. You don't want to cause your left shoulder to "overclimb" through impact.

Note: to clear up any possible misconception, I have not said that the first move in the downswing is made by the right shoulder. The downswing starts with the hips or lower body center moving toward the target. The shoulder motion, good or bad, is a responsive motion that ties in with the hips or lower body.

In a model swing, the hands and arms are passive during this step and respond to rather than initiate any action. The right elbow gives the appearance of attaching to, then being glued to, the right side just above the right hip area. The left arm is fully extended from the body—straight. It is here that good players feel pull, but that is only a sensation, not a result of any conscious pull with the hands or arms. With your right elbow glued to your right side and your left arm straight, it is easy to see that Step Five is a very powerful position. Your hands and arms have not "run off" but are simply responding accurately and appropriately to the body motions. The clubshaft is very close to the same position it was in at Step Three—exceptions include ninety degrees of angle or more with the left arm and clubshaft. The downswing is inside (narrower than) the backswing. (This is one of my fundamentals.) Your wrists are in a fully cocked position. The club should not be outside your hands unless you intend to hit a cut. If it is outside the hands, this is a perfect illustration of "casting" (starting the release motion too soon) or exaggerating the initial rotation of the shoulders. The *"delivery position,"* as I call it, will always show you the golfer's impact position. It is a critical spot in the swing that determines all ball flight. It is always a position I carefully analyze in my teaching.

At Step Five, body weight has shifted back noticeably to the left. It has recentered the body and weight is shifting forward and *diagonally left.*

Your belt buckle as viewed from the front has slid seven to twelve inches toward the target, from Step Four to Step Six. This slide is a natural response to the lower body—the feet and legs—initiating the downswing. It happens *automatically* in a sequenced swing. If you monitor the belt buckle on any top player, you'll immediately see this powerful lateral movement.

At Step Five, the shaft should have traveled down along a path that, when viewed down the target line, is between the tip of your shoulder and your right elbow. If the shaft stays in this Corridor of Success with the butt end of the club pointing to an extension of the ball-to-target line, this indicates an on-plane swing and promising solid contact and good trajectory.

In viewing the swings of the amateurs I teach, I sometimes see the shaft improperly low—dropped beneath the elbow. In this case, the dotted line from the shaft butt hits the ground at a point well beyond the target line. From this position you will push or hook the ball—if you make solid contact. Often, you will hit behind the ball from this inside, shallow swing arc.

SEEING IS BELIEVING

When viewing your swing at Step Five, in a mirror or on a high-quality video player, check to see that your clubface is square or slightly open. Having the clubface in the proper position at this point allows you to pour on the heat—to release everything in a natural manner without fear of hitting a nightmare hook. A sure Death Move is to have the clubface in a severely shut or severely open position at Step Five.

A far more common problem I witness is indicated when the shaft moves downward on a path that takes it above the tip of the shoulder. In this instance, a line drawn from the butt of the club would point to the player's feet. We call this "shaft tip over." From this position at Step Five, you will usually contact the ball with the toe of the clubface and hit a weak slice—Death Position! If you manage to square the clubface, you'll pull the ball. Finally, this move is also characteristic of the shank.

STEP FIVE: FINAL CHECKPOINTS

1. The right knee has kicked forward (toward the ball or target line), and there is a substantial space between your knees.

2. The hips have shifted a few inches, in response to your weight-shifting action, and reached the square position. The shoulders trail the hips.

3. The head has stabilized at, or slightly behind, its address position.

4. The right heel is grounded or, at most, slightly off the ground. At this point in the swing, it should never be extra high.

5. The flexed left knee is forward of your left hip. The left knee is more or less in a straight line with the middle of your left foot. The left leg is still flexed but is in the process of straightening.

6. The body has entered the classic "sit-down" position many players and teachers have long observed.

7. The clubshaft is on plane.

8. The shoulders are unwinding at a rapid pace, yet still lag your hips in rotation. The golf swing depends heavily on "connection," but in the downswing we also see two instances of *separation*—first, the lower body "leaves" the shoulders, then the hands and arms "separate" from the shoulders. The distance between your hands and right shoulder increases as the club reaches our "delivery position."

9. The right arm should be slightly visible under your left starting down.

10. Your eyes are fixed on the ball.

11. The clubhead is behind your body.

12. Many golfers will benefit by *slowing down* the turn back to the target. Sometimes it is useful to slow the upper torso—other times the lower—and sometimes both.

13. A big secret to good shot making is the clubshaft position at Step Five and the square orientation of the clubface. I call this "the delivery position."

14. Supinate the left wrist on the downward move. This happens during Step Five. Sometimes we actually teach this move. That is making the left wrist flat or slightly bowed. If the wrists, hands, and clubhead truly respond to the lower body this flattening should happen with no conscious thought. When it does not happen, we teach it. When you stop the club at Step Five, check your left wrist position. It must not be cupped.

1. The clubshaft is "tipped over" or above your right shoulder, or the clubshaft is directly above your hands.

2. The clubshaft has dropped under your right elbow and is parallel to the ground (or almost parallel); your right palm faces the sky.

3. The head is facing toward the target or your eyes have moved off the ball.

4. The body slides or drifts too far past the ball. This is caused by your weight sliding left too early. It is most visible in the upper body. When the legs go dead, the upper body will usually slide ahead.

5. The clubface is extremely open or closed.

THE SIT-DOWN (FOR ADVANCED PLAYERS ONLY)

All powerful throwing motions proceed in a sequence of weight shift, rotation, arm swing—or "shift-rotate-throw." In all such acts, the quality of the sequence affects final impact speed tremendously. In the golf swing, "sitting down" at the right time recenters weight just as the swing's most dramatic and important weight transfer is about to take place. (The start of the downswing.)

The sit-down is subtle, but feeling your left knee move back toward the target in a *half-circle motion*, feeling your right knee *kicking* at the golf ball, feeling a *push* off your right instep, or feeling your left hip start its *rotation* back toward the target will allow you to understand it better. It can also be felt as a split-second recentering of the body before the full power rotation into impact, and beyond. *At this position, a good checkpoint is to see if your thighs and knees are parallel to the target line.*

The sit-down can be encouraged and practiced, but it does not occur at a static, isolated moment, such that it can be attended to before the golfer moves on to striking the golf ball. It is simply a position you *move through* in the golf swing. It is also something you must practice to help your body understand the correct movements. The continued rotation of the hips, the firing of the right side, the commitment forward to the finish position automatically straightens up the braced left side of the body. The left leg will be straight or nearly straight at impact. From sit-down, we will move toward *stand-up*. This is natural and will happen automatically with correct hip action, since the hip line does rise for all top players from address to impact.

The sit-down is a big key to hitting the ball powerfully. To master it, think *lower body resistance and then lower body initiation*. Practice a right arm (sidearm) throwing motion, such as you would use to skip a flat rock across a pond or lake. Last, constantly examine your swing in a mirror. Make normal and slow-motion swings without a club to get your body actions into correct sequence. Make some incorrect motions on purpose, then compare the feel of them with the proper motion. You will most likely need to consult the services of a top teaching professional to get this absolutely right. If done correctly, this motion tremendously helps put the arms and club into our perfect "delivery position."

Warning: as the change of direction is initiated via the lower body, the hands, wrists, and arms are passive. A likely cause of missing the sit-down motion is that your hands, wrists, and arms become active, without your lower body moving. The result: the throw is preceding the shift and the rotation. *When sequence is destroyed, loss of power and off-center hits ensue.*

A related problem is the initiation of the downswing with the upper body, the shoulders in particular. Results: your hands are thrown much too far outward, the club does not fall in, and the downswing is too steep and too out-to-in.

PUMP DRILL

As you have read in my explanation to Step Five, this to me is the make-or-break move in golf; therefore, this drill could be the most important drill you practice in golf. Pump the club to the delivery position in Step Five. Getting to great delivery really separates the men and boys, and good ball strikers from someone who is totally inconsistent. It is worth the effort to master this drill and practice it often. From the top of your backswing, pump the club down to the halfway position. When you do it, you must *make sure to do it correctly. This drill has to be executed really well.* You have to get the club lined up with the target or parallel to the target line. In addition, the clubface must be in a square position, the toe up position. We can get away with its being somewhat closed in the backswing but when we come down I want the clubface square. I also want the right elbow to return to the right side and just in front of the right hip, and I also want you to be into the sit-down position described earlier, where your weight is again evenly distributed or slightly forward. At this stage, your upper center must not be ahead of your lower center. Your upper center is not even on top of your lower center, it is still trailing. There is still an axis tilt of the spine away from the target as you start down.

Now, understand that this can be overdone. You have to be very careful your spine is not leaning back too far. Your head will have returned very close to its address position, so if there was some shift of the head to the right on the backswing, there should be close to that amount of shift back, which is a very natural move. When you are looking in a mirror you can easily see what is happening. You must not let your head shift ahead of its address position. If it shifts slightly behind that line, you are probably okay. So we go up to the top and pump the club down and repeat. Do it often. This is a wonderful drill to do at home in front of a mirror. You can get a tremendous amount done at home, and you can also use this pump drill at the range. I have some students pump the club down to that halfway down position several times, then hit a golf ball. So the pump drill is from Step Four to Step Five from the top of the backswing to delivery. Take the club up to the top and stop, pump, and then go back to Step Four, top of the backswing. You go from position four to position five and then from position five wind it back up to four, then back down to five. Go from the top of the backswing to delivery over and over until you get that great sequence feel and the great feeling of the club lowering or dropping into that hitting slot. It is a super drill.

STEP SIX: IMPACT

At last: the *moment of truth*. If you consistently arrive at the impact position with the proper alignments and sufficient clubhead speed, whatever your swing looked like getting there is *irrelevant*. Whatever small mistakes and swing flaws you committed along the way are forgiven.

Any player who can arrive at an excellent impact position consistently with speed has what we all strive so hard to achieve: a repeating (therefore, *perfect*) swing—for that player. The look of a swing is, in the final analysis, overrated. Why else would we see so many champion golfers with highly individualized swing characteristics? The most important characteristic they share is this: they all arrive in the impact position with the same solid consistency.

I have spent long hours minutely comparing the swings of top players and have come to this conclusion: any accomplished player, including such unconventional swingers as Lanny Wadkins, Bruce Lietzke, Lee Trevino, and Sergio Garcia, stretch the parameters of preference to the outer limits. But would they have been better players following some "perfect model"? I think not. We probably would never have heard of them. That natural brilliance of a gifted athlete should not be removed if he or she consistently gets to Step Six. Ironically, at Step Six—impact—differences fall away and common points abound. For example, each clubface is square, each player's angle of attack is on plane,

LEFT
Step Six: Front

RIGHT
Step Six: Back

the ball contact is on the center of the clubface, and the clubhead speeds are all high. And the left and right hands of these players are working as a tight unit, not fighting each other. By the way, a wonderful sensation to feel at impact is that of the right side "firing" fully and the clubface *covering the ball*. Jimmy Ballard has long used this phrase to express the feeling you get when contact is flush and the clubhead and ball seem to be united along the target line for an extra split second.

RIGHT
Step Six: Two Views

Here are some vital facts about impact:

- The left wrist must be flat or slightly arched (or bowed, or supinated) at Step Six. The worst power loss you can experience is the inward collapsing of the left wrist at impact. Common causes of this power loss are a slowing down of the hands through impact—which happens when a player attempts to steer the clubhead into the back of the ball—or overacceleration of the clubhead—in which the right hand causes the clubhead to run out ahead of the hands before impact. In a still photograph, you would see that overacceleration causes the clubshaft to line up with the right arm rather than the left arm, as it should. Both conditions result in a great loss of power. They are not often discussed, but these two swing malfunctions are terribly common among high-handicap golfers.

- The right wrist must be angled at impact, not straight, to match up with the flat left wrist. The angle of the right wrist is one of the very few characteristics that replay the look of the address position. Therefore, the right wrist must not hinge forward. The hands and wrists must work together throughout the swing, and they can't if the right wrist hinges independently.

- The left arm and clubshaft, when viewed from above, should line up with each other. The shaft cannot lag too far behind the left arm, nor can it pass the left arm before impact. Both of these conditions indicate serious mistiming of the swing.

- Weight has transferred to the left leg and is on the left foot, more toward the heel. The right heel is one to four inches off the ground; some players will feel a push off the right foot—an excellent key, by the way.

- The right knee has fired forward at Step Six, up to about your body centerline. An effective timing key is to think, "Right knee and hands back to the ball together." The left knee will still have a slight flex to it. The legs are spaced apart from one another, rather than having the right leg passing over and catching the left; if this happens, the probable cause is too narrow a stance, too much hip action, or overly fast feet and leg action.

- There is space between the legs.

- The right elbow is very close to the right hip and still shows a slight bow.

- The right heel is ahead of the right toe.

- The chin has returned to its starting position or is now

pointing toward the ball. (On wood shots, the head may be slightly behind where it started.)

- The hips and shoulders have maintained some spacing and a degree of separation. In other words, the hips are leading the shoulders and the shoulders must not catch up to the hips. What the hips have done is clear well to the left (twenty degrees) as a result of proper rotation. The shoulders will also be slightly left at impact, ten to twenty degrees. *Remember:* it is far easier to slide the hips toward the target than it is to rotate them clear to the left—don't get sloppy and just "hip slide" forward.

- The body stands up a little bit at impact. That's because we are using the ground as leverage to get power into the swing. Your hip line should be higher at impact than at address.

- The right elbow is slightly bent at impact. It is only after impact that the right arm fully straightens.

DEEP "TOE-DEEP" DIVOTS WITH THE SHAFT VERY STEEP AT IMPACT

During the downswing, many beginners have a tendency to employ the Death Move of swinging the right arm out and away from the body. In effect, the typical novice throws the clubhead at the ball.

Because impact occurs in an instant (0.0004 second), it may seem odd to devote great attention to it. Indeed, some students find it difficult to think about impact. Yet I've found that working back from the perfect alignments of impact is an excellent teaching technique. Visualizing a perfect impact position and making lots of practice swings that stop at impact helps you feel the sensation of a good impact position.

Before I move on to Step Seven, a note on head movement is called for here. Some golfers' heads, at the time of impact of club and ball, will have moved rearward and slightly behind their original address positions. Unquestionably, the head moves during the golf swing. Trying to freeze your head in one location can be a poor idea. *Typically, the head moves forward because your legs don't.* When you succeed in locking your head into position throughout the swing, you generally create trouble for yourself in other areas. The head reacts very naturally to the forces built up as a result of the motion and turning of the body. To attempt to restrict it completely is counterproductive. So, allow your head its natural motion—just keep your eyes focused on the ball until impact.

THE PINCH DRILL

This is part of our chip, pinch, punch sequence that we teach people at our schools. The pinch is a small swing where we squeeze or pinch the golf ball off the turf and then hold right after impact. You make a small swing and then, *boom*, you pinch the ball and hold the finish in a very short position. When you hold it, here's what we're looking for: *a flat left wrist* for the right hander and the *club pointed back in center* and also *the left arm (the lead arm) must be connected* (that means the upper left arm is attached to the upper left part of your body). I am just talking about the upper left arm—not from the elbow up, but about halfway up from your left arm to the top of your left side. Now a lot of people will go through impact and disconnect. Also, the club may be out of center; it is easy to be out of center by flipping the hands. The left wrist breaks down going through, the right wrist straightens out. That is the worst possible mistake to make and the biggest power leak you could have. Or you might overdrag the club and have the grip end of the club pointing outside your body. Another very bad mistake is a sawing action going the impact zone, where the left elbow breaks down and the club gets sucked in across the golf ball in a swiping or swing action.

A lot of things can go wrong, but the pinch drill allows you to see easily whether you did it or did not do it. There is no in-between here. When you do this pinch drill, you will be practicing great alignments. You will have to use good footwork, good weight shift, and achieve solid impact positioning, which you hold in the pinch. When you do it and squeeze the ball out there, you will be stunned at how far the golf ball goes and how solid it feels. It is a great drill! The pinch drill will teach you where you need to be at impact, what great impact feels like, and also what great impact looks like, just past the impact position.

STEP SEVEN: EARLY FOLLOW-THROUGH

Step Seven of the golf swing is the segment between impact and the point at which your right arm is parallel to the ground. Some of the poor positioning and mistakes that occur at this point are the outgrowth of much earlier errors and problems, but other Step Seven mistakes crop up during and right after impact. The most notable problems at this stage tend to stem from a break-down of the connection between the left shoulder and the left side of the chest. *This is perhaps the most important connection point of the swing,* and letting it break apart leads to two major flaws:

- The hands and the club overextend down the target line, the left arm disconnects from the left side, and the left wrist breaks down completely. When this happens, the left shoulder remains in view (to a face-on observer) long past the point at which it should no longer be visible. A hook, push, or flyer shot usually results.
- The left elbow slides across the body in a sawing motion; in a face-on view, the left shoulder disappears from view prematurely, the left arm breaks down, the left elbow points up toward the sky.

Thanks to the symmetry that is inherent in a sound golf swing, certain aspects of a proper Step Seven will mirror the good things seen in Step Five. For example, a good player's elbows and forearms will be nearly level to one another at this juncture, just as they were at the equivalent point of the downswing. (Here you can lay a yardstick or a golf club across your forearms to test for levelness.) Slightly further in the follow-through, an imaginary beam of light emanating from the butt end of the shaft will point directly at the ball-to-target line during the follow-through, just as it did at a corresponding phase of the downswing.

Looking up the target line at the golfer as he or she completes Step Seven, you should observe that the line of the clubshaft extends out from the line of the right arm with only a slight angle at the hands. I've noticed the good player's clubshaft makes an unbroken straight line with the right arm, just past this checkpoint position. Moreover, the continuing rotation of the

TAKE THE TRIANGLE TEST

As a drill, practice retaining the important connections of your swing by checking the distance between the butt of the club and your navel. See that this gap does not decrease from impact through Step Seven.

Another important check involves the orientation of the club handle within the all-important triangle formed by your arms and your shoulder line. The club should remain in the center of the triangle through this phase of the swing. It should be like a spoke of a wheel, with the center of your abdomen acting as the hub. When the great Roberto de Vicenzo told me he "hit the ball with his stomach," it allowed me to appreciate the idea of proper *connection* through impact.

hips and body center through impact allows the golfer to remain connected through Step Seven.

This is also a point in the swing at which good footwork and legwork can sometimes bog down. Keep your legs and feet driving off the earth and with your body weight moving to its eventual point of total transfer to the left post, or left pivotal point of the swing (your left leg). The right heel is well off the ground.

NEGATIVES TO AVOID

Left Shoulder Climb.   Keep your shoulders level and turning on your spine tilt. In other words, avoid the classic "rock and block."

Eyes Glued Too Long to the Spot.   Once the ball is struck, you have no reason to keep focusing on the divot or tee: in fact, you will contribute to a breakdown of your overall swing if you don't allow your head and eyes to follow the ball once it is away. Ideally, the club is moving at a high rate of speed through impact. Trying to stay down too long will eventually cause you to experience back problems.

Legs Gone Dead as Follow-through Begins. Impact does not mean the legs have completed their task. Keep the weight moving and your footwork and legwork active. Keep your center, or your belt-buckle area, moving. This rotation through impact is very important. Facing the ball too long will disconnect the arms and promote incorrect body action.

Step Seven: Two Views. Notice that you see no arms and no club in the photo on the right. The club shaft will exit in the boxed-in corridor.

THE BEST DRILL
LEFT ARM ONLY

In this seemingly simple drill, you use just your left arm, and it is practiced without the club and with the club.

First, we must learn to do it without the club, and as you know, I am a fanatic on doing these drills correctly. Pay close attention as you practice your left-arm-only drill. When you take the left arm back, you must start down with our correct

POCKET DRILL

If you are concerned that the full body action of your golf swing is insufficient, you should work on the full-swing turn-back-and-through motions with your arms crossed over your chest.

In doing this drill, focus on your right hip pocket (RHP) and your left hip pocket (LHP). The fact is, at the finish, you have to get your right pocket to the spot where your left pocket was at address. Drill this motion whenever you get a chance.

sequence, which is a little shift. You might feel your left hand and your left knee working together, or your left hand and both knees working together, or your left hand and your right knee working together, but you will feel a little synchronization of your lower body action and the left arm working here. That is your little start-down key. As you come through impact, your left wrist must be in its flat impact position. This is the key to Step Seven. The release of left wrist and forearm is done with a rotation of the lower forearm (called the radius). After impact we go into a hitchhiking position, which means the left thumb is angled upward at the sky and the left arm is close to the body. There will be some break in the left elbow, but the left arm will stay connected to the left side and must not increase in length. You must not disconnect the left arm from the left upper quadrant of your body, and the invisible club that we are using will be pointed at the target line. Now this drill is not left-arm-only, it is left arm and body together. There is coordination or synchronization, *a connection of the left arm and the body action when done correctly*. When you put the golf club in your hand, you absolutely have to use your body to hit the golf ball, at least to hit it with any kind of distance.

I have watched Johnny Miller do this drill for many years and he can hit a 7 iron 160 yards with his left arm only. I have seen a lot of other players do this. It takes a tremendous amount of work, yet I would like you to eventually be able to just clip the ball off a tree and hit it 15–20 yards. That would be great. If you can do that and do it consistently, you will have really learned how to use your left arm correctly.

Remember, you do not need a club. You should do this drill in front of a mirror to see how well you are doing. You must have good forearm rotation going through the golf shot to have the upper arm work correctly and for it to stay connected and coordinated with body shift and body turn. This is a super simple move when it is done right.

STEP EIGHT: FINISH AND REBOUND

In the final phase of the swing, your momentum takes you to a completed follow-through position. Your hips and shoulders are fully rotated and the club is behind your head momentarily, before it returns to a relaxed, balanced position in front of your body. From this position, you just watch the ball travel to its landing area. The return of the club from behind your head is called a *rebound* or reflex action. This is the area I call "hit and evaluate." When you hit, hold, and evaluate your shot, you are accomplishing three important things: optimum *balance*, optimum *feedback*, and optimum *feel*.

Because all the motion of the swing is over, the finish and rebound are fairly easy aspects of your own swing to establish and evaluate. In a mirror, you should see, for example, that your right shoulder finished closer to your target than your left shoulder. And, as you return the club to a waist-high position on the

LEFT
Step Eight: Front

RIGHT
Step Eight: Back

COMMON SWING MISCONCEPTIONS AND FALLACIES

1. There is one swing tip that will be your personal "secret" and you will never be able to overemphasize it.
2. You should play every shot off your left heel.
3. Place your weight out toward your toes at address.
4. Your arms should hang straight down from your shoulders when you set up.
5. All good players have good grips.
6. Barely grasp the club with your right hand.
7. Keep your head up at address.
8. Keep your head down throughout the motion.
9. Keep your left arm straight.
10. When your wrists are cocked at the halfway point of the backswing, the butt of the club should point at the ball.
11. A closed clubface at the top of the backswing automatically leads to hooking.
12. Pull the club down to the ball with your left arm.

rebound, you should feel that your grip pressure there, as well as at the finish, is no weaker than it was at impact. You haven't lost anything off your grip pressure, in other words. Your basic grip/hand position from address is the same.

If you are looking in a mirror that is pointed at you from the target area, you should notice that the clubshaft crosses through your head at the full-finish position. Its plane may well match the plane of your shoulders. I don't like to see the club flopped vertically over your shoulders like a heavy laundry bag.

During the downswing, weight travels across your feet in a rolling action. The front foot holds its basic position, as a brace against the force of the body, arms, and club as you contact the ball. If you spin your front foot from its original orientation—so that it ends up more or less parallel with the target line—your swing will be out of control and you'll lose power. This counter-clockwise turning of the left foot after impact is usually a compensation for poor balance earlier in the swing and indicates a spinout. Ironically, this unorthodox "foot fault" will help you regain balance as you move to the top of the finish, but the spinout is a bad sign. No top player makes this move. If anything, great players—Jack Nicklaus and Greg Norman, for example—may actually move their left heel forward, toward the target on the downswing, to brace themselves further and to provide a force to "hit against."

By making a balanced, athletic swing and holding your connections together, you can hit a big golf shot and finish at an exact stop without forcing it. Many great players practice by swinging full and holding their finishes like statues. Normally, the only time you will see a tour pro incapable of holding his or her finish is when he or she has made a hard swing from a dramatically uneven lie, such as on the wall of a bunker. But the poor player shows this fidgety, teetering finish on shots from flat ground. Avoid this and be conscious of balance.

RIGHT ARM AND SHAFT DRILL

This is one of our classic drills. We have the student swing a shaft with right arm only (if you are a left hander do this drill with your left hand). What we do here is get a simple right-sided underhanded toss going, just as if you are throwing the shaft down the fairway. The club should whistle through the air and finish on the shoulder. Get it right and you will have flexibility or mobility in the wrists that you need to play golf. Most golfers are too tight in the wrist to get the whistle in the shaft. When they first do it they may throw the club early. Instead you want the whistle or your speed at the bottom or even just past the impact area. The whistle must not occur too early in your swing as some people tend to do.

13. Your head is the axis point of the swing, and it should stay still throughout the swing.
14. The right hand or right arm causes hooking.
15. Swing the club down the target line.
16. Finish high.

LEFT
Right Arm Drill

OPPOSITE
Step Eight: Finish (top) and rebound (bottom).

This seemingly simple drill is not that easy. Like all the drills, it must be done correctly to be effective. Follow the instructions carefully, look at the picture, and practice this. You could actually do this with a fairly good size rope the length of a club. You could also do it with a wispy branch that has some flexibility to it. You could do it with a shaft, like we use at the school. A driver length shaft works really well; it is a little bit longer, and it makes a loud whistle when you do it. When you finish the swish, make sure your eyes are at the target, make sure you can tap your back foot, and also make sure that shaft hits your shoulder like Fred Couples, Davis Love, or Ernie Els, who all finish their swings this relaxed way. When you have the correct action, your hand will be about 6–8 inches away from your shoulder. Your hand actually will not be resting on your shoulder nor will it be too far away. The shaft finishes on your shoulder with the right wrist fully recocked.

An Addition to the Right Arm and Shaft Drill. We advance this drill by adding a step. We start with a reasonably narrow stance with the feet 8–12 inches apart. Then as you get the club away about waist high (as the club is still going back), take a step forward. That gives you the two-way direction action that a good player has. The club will respond to the step, so when you do this right, the shaft will be going away from the target as you make a step forward and then swing. Step, swing, and finish. This drill, just an addition to the right arm and shaft drill, really gives you the tremendous feel of how the body leads the downswing.

THE TWO-STEP AND THE FOUR-STEP SWING

Practice Steps for Beginner and Advanced Students

WHY EIGHT STEPS

This is a good question, and the answer came from using a sequence camera during the 1970s when I taught at Westchester Country Club. Previously I had watched Carly Welty use this camera and also Ben Doyle (who taught the super technical "Golf Machine"), when he taught out in California. I took numerous lessons from Ben, and I thought the sequence camera was phenomenal. The eight sequential pictures of your swing were ready to be looked at in one minute. (There was no video at this time.) I bought a sequence camera as soon as I began teaching in 1975.

A dial lets you time the swing to get different sections photographed. I got pretty good at timing the whole sequence and used it in every lesson (and learned that every swing is slightly different). That timing device on the sequence camera is very sensitive, so you could move it to get any segment of the swing. If you did it right, you could get the backswing portions and the downswing portions; it would take eight frames. Often I could get four back and four through. I would write my notes on the back of the photo and give it to my students. I also learned to look for certain positions and common errors. Eight stuck with me as a great number. It gives you four backswing positions and four downswing positions. That is how I came up with my eight-step checkpoint positions for video review.

You realize that I do not usually try to teach all eight steps. It is a fact that we almost never teach all eight steps at any school, but we do use the eight steps as instructors to analyze the golf swing. As we teach the positions to our students, we will often divide the groups into different categories or levels of players. For some players (beginning players) we use two steps. We called that the two-step golf swing.

TWO, FOUR, SIX BEFORE EIGHT

THE TWO-STEP

1. Halfway back
2. Finish

By teaching just two positions, the beginning golfer has two places they know they need to get. The positions are specific, easy to remember, and easy to practice. The halfway back position, by the way, has been taught for about five hundred years. If you make a serious mistake early in your backswing it is likely you will never recover. We teach this move by focusing on the golf club, hands, and arms. When the club, hands, and arms get into a good position, going back, we can really help that person. We stop them and work with them until they set the proper extension with the clubface in a toe-up position (see Steps Two, Four, and Six in Chapter 4). With the hands over the right foot with the left arm and the clubshaft being fairly closely aligned we are in good shape.

THE FINISH POSITION

I love to get players in good balance in the finish of their golf swing and in a solid finish position.

These two positions are great for all beginning players. This is something they can work on and learn where they need to be. At the finish of the golf swing I want them fully over the front leg, on the right toe, balanced on their front leg, standing tall, and their eyes looking level at the target, the hands and arms like in the picture on page 101. Also they need to have the same grip pressure from the start to halfway back, and through to the finish. This may seem easy, but it is a very difficult thing for the beginning golfer to do. It takes a tremendous amount of golf swings. You can practice this at home or in your backyard. This practice will help any beginning golfer into the intermediate level. Learning to finish in this fashion often has a very positive effect on the overall swing with no conscious thought by the student.

THE FOUR-STEP SWING

I wrote about this earlier. I call these the four basic steps, and they can be learned in fifteen minutes, by anybody. Once you know them, then of course it takes time to make them part of your swing. You will really need to work hard on your own to accomplish these four positions. You are going to have to read this often and study the book carefully. I want to say up front it is not easy to read something out of a book and then execute what the writer actually wants, but it can be done. So here we go. Get yourself into the four basic positions. Two back and two through.

1. Halfway back. Critical position (same as Step Two).
2. Full backswing. Loaded up on back leg. Turned behind the golf ball. Balance on the inside part of your back leg and coiled behind the golf ball. Remember to stay in the framework you set at address. By this I mean staying level with your tilt and head position throughout the backswing. (See Step Four in Chapter 4.)

3.   Impact. The moment of truth. Impact happens in a microsecond. So many people ask, Why would you teach something that happens in such a short period of time? Well, because impact is so different from address. I think it is very important for people to understand where they want to be when they strike the golf ball. We do this very slowly, and we repeat it many times. We actually have many people start at address and then go to impact with no backswing at all. Get into a good address position and then shift their body to a good impact position, address to impact. As you study the eight steps you will see in detail just how different you need to be at impact from your starting position. Virtually everything is different. For right now, to understand more clearly, I recommend you study Step Six in Chapter 4. You can see the golfer has approximately 75 percent of the weight on his front foot. You can see that he has rolled off the inside of his back foot and there is some air underneath the back heel. The right knee is kicked forward. The left arm and the golf club are in line, the head is behind the golf ball, and the back shoulder is lower than the left shoulder. The hips—the center of your body—are turned toward the target between a range of ten degrees open to maybe eighty degrees open. I prefer the hips in the range of ten to forty degrees open.

4.   Finish. See finish in two-step swing. It is position eight on page 101.

We have also kept our hands together with no change in grip pressure. What is different is that the left wrist, for the right hander, has flattened and the right wrist is cocked. The right wrist is bent backward more than it was at address. This is very important and is quite different from what most people believe. I show people a drill; I have them hold a club against a tree or against the end of the mat. Feel pressure in the shaft as if the club is going into the ground. Of course the concept is basically striking the ball, then going into the ground, taking a divot to compress the golf ball. It is a tremendously important position, so you cannot overdo the practice of going from the top of the backswing, slowly down through impact, and holding.

Repeat, top of back to impact, and from there we go from impact all the way to the finish, which in the four-step swing is position four. We actually hold the impact position and then swing the club very slowly to the great finish position. We talked about the finish in the more simple two-step, same finish, same balance, with the eyes at the target and the back heel completely off the ground balanced on the back toe, weight totally on the forward foot.

Now let's run through the swing, *from setup, go to position one halfway back, then position two top of backswing, three impact, and four finish*. That is the four-step swing. Those are what we call the basic positions. It is a wonderful way to learn the golf swing, and in a very basic way it is half of the Eight-Step Swing. Most can get a new understanding of the golf swing in steps or pieces and they learn what should be happening. This will accelerate how quickly you improve as a player.

BODY MOTIONS FOR ADVANCED GOLF

A Teacher's Guide to Diagnosis, Including Excellent Drills to Counteract Death Moves

My usual approach to working with *intermediate to advanced* players is to make sure that they mentally understand, and physically feel, the basic elements of the backswing and downswing *pivot* actions. These actions, involving particularly the feet, knees, hips, shoulders, and head, comprise the nucleus of the swing in that they allow a player to move the club back properly to the top and then deliver it squarely and powerfully into the back of the ball, without any conscious manipulation of the hands being necessary. Essentially, the pivot is what allows the entire swing motion to operate virtually on *automatic pilot*. For this reason, I will now describe and break down the vital elements of the pivot in the simplest possible manner. Understanding them will expedite the learning process and ready you for the more sophisticated steps of the swing, which will be presented in Chapter 7.

THE BACKSWING PIVOT

ELEMENT ONE: FOOTWORK

Tremendous emphasis is placed on your connection to the club—your grip—but what about your grip on the ground? Think about it: much of the power you apply to the golf ball traces itself back to the resistance point between your feet and the ground. Good footwork is necessary in all sports and certainly in the exe-

cution of an effective golf swing. When your footwork is right, your lower body resistance is sound as well.

Good footwork is athletic in appearance throughout the swing. It is lively, efficient, and powerful. During the setup, the weight is equally balanced on your feet. However, it should never favor being forward toward the toes. If anything, the weight is more toward the heels than the toes. As the backswing starts,

FOOTWORK FAULTS

Poor footwork usually runs toward either of two extremes:

1. An absence of footwork—golfer glued to the ground.
2. The golfer's left heel lifts early, with the weight too far forward.

The "flat foot" plants all twenty-two spikes in the ground and doesn't let go, causing the arms to flail away at the ball. The "tap dancer" is up on the toes of the left foot early in the backswing, causing a lower body sway or overrotation of the knees.

Check carefully for footwork faults.

there is first a feeling of slight weight shift off the inside of the left instep, with a constant increase of weight shift to the inside of the right foot (*toward the right heel*) and right leg. I like to see the weight shift occur early as the clubhead travels away from the target.

It is fine, on long shots, for the left heel to come off the ground during a full backswing if it is *pulled* off the ground by the force of your weight shift and pivot. It is not fine for the left heel to be lifted off the ground voluntarily, as an unconnected act. If it does rise, and I think it can on long shots, the left heel should never go more than a few inches off the ground. Many top players keep the left heel on the ground even for a full drive.

ELEMENT TWO: KNEE ACTION

Your knee action and knee turn will, to a large degree, dictate the amount of hip rotation you ultimately make. Freeze your knees, and your hips will be "frozen" as well—they *can't* pivot! If you employ too much knee action or knee turn, your hips will be free to overrotate. There will be no lower body resistance, thus you will have great difficulty returning to proper impact alignments. (Exaggerated knee action is very common among high-handicap golfers.)

Proper knee motion involves both knees. On the backswing, the left knee breaks inward and outward simultaneously. It simply stays in sync with the total release of the entire left side in your take-away. The danger occurs when the left knee travels too far in either direction. Too much left knee movement causes slack in the legs and often results in a lower body slide. Don't allow the left knee to pass your spine or your centerline. (The modern golf backswing action is usually characterized by "quiet" knee and leg action.)

ABOVE

Controlled knee action is a key to both resistance and rotation.

The right knee action is critical to the bracing of the entire right leg and hip. The right knee does not freeze, and it is definitely a plus if you can maintain your flex throughout the backswing. *The Death Move for the right knee is sliding.* When the right knee slides, your weight will move incorrectly to the outside of the right leg and your lower body resistance will diminish greatly. So, in effect, you "post up" against the braced right knee in a solid backswing.

Element Three: Hip Action

The lower body should resist the turning of the upper body during the backswing (to create torque), then initiate the downswing by releasing that torque. Think of it as a spring being wound in your hips and torso, then unwound with a torquing power that accelerates the shoulders, arms, and club. Less hip movement on the backswing usually translates into a more powerful movement on the forward swing.

RIGHT
Top players realize that hip action is a vital link to power.

I must caution you that resistance in the hips can be overdone. When the knees freeze, the hips cannot turn. So the knees must rotate some to allow the hips to rotate. I routinely see students who need more hip turn. Either they lack rotation of the knees or they slide the knees and hips back. There must be some turn over the right leg. The right hip must go back around. The Corridor of Success ranges from approximately forty to forty-five degrees of hip turn for the very supple player to sixty to sixty-five for the less flexible who cannot make a full shoulder turn without the extra hip rotation. It is just a fact that I see far more students who overturn and overwork the knees and the hips on the backswing than do it correctly. Thus lower body resistance is usually a great thought to have in mind if you want to pivot correctly and, in turn, increase both your power and your accuracy.

Element Four: Shoulder Movement

The shoulders, arms, and hands start the backward movement of the club away from the ball and the shoulders make the biggest turn in the backswing. It's often useful to visualize the shoulders turning twice as much as the hips. On a full driver swing, you might see your critical body motions in the following terms: the knees turn twenty-five degrees and the hips fifty degrees, while the shoulders turn one hundred degrees.

The shoulders turn on an axis. Again, it is useful to see your shoulders rotating on their own plane. Your "spine angle" at address determines the shoulder axis.

The shoulders must not turn level like a merry-go-round, which will bring the arms and club too far inside and around. Conversely, they must not overtilt like a Ferris wheel, which causes the swing to be too vertical.

When you correctly turn your shoulders, you feel as if your right shoulder were going up and behind your head, while your left shoulder traveled level and behind the ball.

It's very possible to overturn the shoulders. On all but the fullest swing, the shoulders will not turn more than ninety degrees. *It is the gap between the shoulders and hips that creates the torque in the body. Therefore, the largest percentage of turn must come from the shoulders.*

When the shoulders overturn, the arms are carried too far and eventually weight begins to "tip over" into the left side. Overrotating the shoulders thus can cause a reverse pivot. The overturn causes a host of other problems, including pulling the head and eyes off the ball and loss of balance. Golfers with this problem need to limit the amount of rotation in the shoulders to gain more power.

ELEMENT FIVE: HEAD MOVEMENT

The head turns and/or moves to the right slightly. It has to, or the pivot will be so tense and mechanical that you will not employ a free, athletic backswing action. In a full swing, a top player rotates the chin to the right twenty to twenty-five degrees. Harvey Penick, the famous teacher, probably put it best: "Show me a player who doesn't move his head, and I'll show you someone who can't play."

Although head movement is a necessary part of the pivot, for best results your eyes should remain focused on the ball. It's the pivot and movement of the head that allow you to make a complete shoulder turn, while freezing the head into a stationary post hinders the turning action of the shoulders, robbing you of vital power. The turn or rotation of the head means there are four specific turns that I look at in the golf swing.

THE DOWNSWING PIVOT

ELEMENT ONE: FOOTWORK

During the downswing, the weight shifts from the right post
to the left post, off the inside of the right foot. This is crucial to
employing the two-pivot-point swing.

The correct right foot and right heel movements reveal what
is occurring with the golfer's weight shift and hip action. In most

ways, the right heel only "reacts" to the body center. As the hips hit the forward wall of lateral shift, there's an abrupt stop. The left leg has firmed and resisted the lateral motion. The hips are in the process of "rising" through impact, and by impact they have also opened to the target. In effect, the turning hips and body center pull the right heel up. This causes a microsecond stop and/or quiver of the right foot. I've never heard anyone mention or write about it, but it definitely does occur during the swings of many of the game's best golfers.

RIGHT
Good footwork on the downswing helps put the club in the perfect delivery position.

Many great players, in particular Sam Snead and Ben Hogan, have used the "push off the right foot" as a tremendous swing key. The right heel kicks forward and toward the ball. On full shots the right heel is off the ground at impact, and the right foot continues to lift until only the toe is touching the ground. I have found it most interesting that many of the all-time greats slide their right foot forward and that their right heel moves up before impact, then moves downward, then back up. This is a clear indication of forward drive, before the player hits the braced-up "wall" of the body's left side. A common thought that many powerful ball hitters use to initiate the downswing is "Replant the left heel."

A common fault of poor footwork is for the left heel to back up on the forward swing. When I see this, I know that the golfer has "spun out." Because the left hip and left heel must work in the same direction, I know that the golfer has spun his or her left hip back.

ELEMENT TWO: KNEE ACTION

The typical amateur has too much knee action in the backswing and too little in the downswing. In contrast, the typical tour professional resists with the lower body, then really uses the ground and the knees to pump forward into the finish.

It doesn't matter which knee triggers the downswing. What's important is that both knees move laterally, then rotate, and at the finish of the swing, virtually touch one another. (In some great swings, the left knee noticeably leads the downswing. However, this move can be overdone, causing an excessive slide.) See page 84, The Sit-Down.

ELEMENT THREE: HIP ACTION

As the right knee moves outward toward the ball, the hips recenter and the right heel rises ever so slightly. Then, as the body's "center" rises through impact and the hips rotate diagonally left, the right heel hesitates or drops down slightly. This unique and very brisk up-and-down movement of the right heel is at least partially triggered by the right knee's changing

direction and moving the way of the rotating hips. It is an interesting observation, but not something you should think about.

As the body fully releases and the player's weight is fully forward, the hips actually turn left of the target. Finally, the player is balanced on his or her right toe, with the knees together and no space at all between the thighs.

On the downswing, the hips slide between seven and twelve inches toward the target in combination with a forceful and powerful hip rotation. Unquestionably, there is *lateral motion*.

Even though the hips lead the shoulders, the more quickly rotating shoulders are able, in effect, nearly to catch up to the hips at impact. Both hips and shoulders are open to the target line at impact, with the hips still ahead and still more open. Make no mistake, however, it's the hips or lower body that lead the parade and provide the initiation of power in the swing.

A final important thought regarding the shoulders is that their motion must be uninterrupted, with no stops or delays at or past impact. Feel the left shoulder continue to rotate left and backward through the ball.

Watch the head movement of a top player during his or her swing. Notice that the chin rotates to the right on the backswing, reenters the address position for a freeze-frame at impact, then rotates toward the target at the finish. As it is pivoting, it may also move laterally—to the right during the backswing and to the left during the forward swing. Like the body as a whole, the head pivots and also moves in creating a powerful swing and shot. The head has a pivot and it moves slightly right and then left to create enough freedom for the shoulders to make a powerful coil.

The head has its own "miniature swing."

ELEMENT FOUR: SHOULDER MOVEMENT

The shoulders must not actually initiate the downswing. The stored energy in the upper torso (created by the gap between the hips and shoulders) plus the work of the lower body will cause the shoulders to unwind with tremendous force. However, the golfer must wait that split second for the lower body to begin the motion. When this occurs, the right shoulder will first lower and then rotate around and forward.

The spine will naturally lean slightly away from the target—slightly more than at the address position. This will be a totally natural occurrence, due completely to the proper sequencing of body motion. It is never something to think about while playing, because it will almost always cause other problems. Rather, the golfer should focus on having the shoulders respond to the lower body. Good footwork causes the shoulders to work correctly.

I have observed that many players tend to lower the right shoulder dramatically; this causes the spine to lean too far back at impact and also promotes an inside-out swing motion. A good swing thought for you is to think *level* on the forward swing with the shoulders. This thought encourages the shoulders to rotate "on plane," or perfectly on their axis.

As the swing is completed, the shoulders will brake and reflex back to a target-facing position. This is a beautifully controlled movement.

ELEMENT FIVE: HEAD MOVEMENT

Around twenty years ago, Johnny Miller (an avid student of the swing) made an offhand comment to me about the head pivoting and having its own swinging motion. I really liked that image and have used it in my teaching ever since. The head has its own miniature swing.

NO PLANE, NO GAIN

The Importance of Swinging the Club on Plane

It's no coincidence that this chapter on swing plane directly follows our discussion of body motion. To swing the club "on plane" throughout the golf swing—powerfully—you must pivot your body properly. *The start of the downswing is the make-or-break point for swing plane. Players who move their bodies in the proper sequence when starting downward movement are much more likely to deliver the clubshaft on plane, swing after swing.*

The actual plane angle of the swing differs from golfer to golfer, because of variances in stature. Plane differs from shot to shot too, because of differences in the lie of the ball and/or the lie angle of the club. All the same, there is still an ironclad cause-and-effect relationship between pivoting properly and swinging powerfully on the established plane. Sequencing the body movements properly allows the club to fall into place much easier without hand or arm manipulation.

As vital as it is, the concept of plane intimidates a lot of golfers. In part, this is because most discussions of swing plane are vague and incomplete. What is it that the golfer should try to swing on plane? The hands? The arms? One answer would be the clubhead. A more accurate answer would be the *clubshaft*. In the process of keeping the clubshaft on plane, the hands, arms, and shoulders might also move on plane. And there will certainly be points in the swing at which the plane established by your left arm or your hands will be the same as the plane the clubshaft moves along. For sure, the hands, arms, and shoulders all play a major role in keeping the clubshaft and clubhead on plane.

LEFT

The McLean Ice Cream Cone:
Combining shaft plane and the
Hogan Plane for a "safety zone."

BODY LINE

TARGET LINE

In many a misleading illustration, the plane of the golf swing is shown as a shadowed area, resembling a sheet of glass, that rests on the golfer's shoulders. Since Ben Hogan's book *Five Lessons* was published in 1957, that imaginary pane of glass has been shown extending upward from the ball through the golfer's hands and passing over the shoulders, with a small hole for his or her head. This classic diagram does *not* tell the whole story of swing plane. It correctly shows the ideal swing plane for the left arm and the clubshaft during the middle period of the swing and up to the top of the backswing. But before you start thinking about whether your swing coincides with this venerable diagram, take a look at another image. What you're looking at in the figure at right is the first plane, or "address plane," of the swing.

RIGHT
The dotted line represents the Address Shaft Plane.

The address plane of the swing is the line we draw along the shaft as it sits at address and might also be termed the "shaft plane." This plane varies somewhat because golfers can hold their hands low or high at address. The shaft angle at impact is also very important but it is an individual matter for a knowledgeable teacher. This plane relates to how the clubhead travels up and down from the ball, to a point that is waist high. In this limited arc, you're either on plane, over the plane, or under the plane. It's one of those three things. One of many statements in Hogan's book about the plane that was completely correct, incidentally, is that the baseline of the swing plane is the line extending from the target back through the ball and continuing farther backward. *That line, the target line, is the most important line in golf* for you as a player. This is the line you use to aim the clubface and set your body angles.

Between the address plane and what we'll call the "Hogan plane," something happens. Your hands, if you were to view them from behind, usually veer upward in a curving path, leaving that lower plane and rising to the Hogan plane. There are exceptions to this rule, but it is still a solid observation.

All in all, there is no question that swing plane is overrated in relation to the backswing. There are many different ways to take the club back that are acceptable. However, I'm all for a simple and direct backswing action. What's important during the take-away are the body movements that get you started and the absence of tension in the arms, wrists, and hands, although the fingers hold the club securely. Of course, if the club goes right up the address shaft plane line, it is tracking back on a model swing arc. However, it is much more important that we do not destroy the naturalness of movement. If the club tends to rise a bit above the address plane line or drop below it slightly, we should have no problem getting to an adequate backswing position. Staying within this liberal Corridor of Success allows you to reach a position of leverage from which you can swing the club powerfully and, most important, on plane in the downswing.

RECONCILING THE TWO PLANES OF THE BACK-SWING WITH THE PLANE OF THE DOWNSWING

Going back to our address shaft plane diagram, we can plot another plane line, one that equates to the plane in Hogan's book. Drawn here on the same page together (see page 126), the two lines form a triangle or ice cream cone, which is an image I picked up in discussions with Denis Pugh, one of Europe's top golf instructors. In evaluating the plane of a student's swing, I check to see if he or she stays within this *safety zone*.

The right elbow is the one part of your body that most tends to sneak out of the safety zone. I don't ever like to see the right elbow underneath the address plane line. That often indicates that the arms have been pulled inside too much or that the right elbow has connected to the body in the backswing and remained connected. This also indicates that the left arm has gone completely across the golfer's chest. All are bad mistakes. These actions violate one of the general principles: *keep the arms in front of your body center throughout the swing.*

You've seen clearly that two separate planes occur in the backswing, and that most golfers elevate their hands (left arm) up and out of the address plane and close to the shoulder plane. You may wonder if a similar lowering and retracking of the hands take place on the downswing. The answer is *no*. For a host of reasons, the plane of the hands in the downswing does not retrack the "ripple," or dish-shaped upward curve, in the middle of the backswing. Gravity, increased swing speed, and the quick lowering motion at the *beginning* of the downswing make the arm-and-hand plane steeper and usually slightly outside the backswing arc. It is also more consistent than the backswing plane and is not dish shaped. Interestingly, the shaft plane works in just the *opposite* way. The plane of the clubshaft actually flattens on the downswing. This mirrors the baseball batter as he or she strides forward into the hitting zone. The baseball bat falls and "flattens" visibly. The top golfers will follow this natural fall-down action as well.

OPPOSITE

Like the baseball batter's plane of swing, the golfer's plane of swing flattens as he moves into the hitting area.

RIGHT

The end of the club that is closer to the ground should point at the target line.

Here are two simple ways for you to think about swing plane and how you can monitor it:

- Remember that the end of the club that is closer to the ground always points to the target line. There are four

ABOVE

An on-plane swing (left); an off-plane swing (right).

important points in a model swing when the shaft is parallel to the target line: halfway back, at the top, halfway down, and halfway up to the follow-through finish. When the club is at address or impact, or near to either, the end of the shaft should point directly at the target line. When the grip end of the club is closer to the ground, the grip end of the shaft should, indeed, be pointed at that target line.

- Check how sensitive the on-plane swing is to small muscle movements by sticking a tee in the vent hole of the grip and slowly swinging the club backward. Stop when your left arm is parallel to the ground and the club is set. Ideally, the tee will be aimed directly at the target line.

A flat backswing axis (left); shoulders turning on the correct axis (right).

Now rotate your wrists just a small amount and notice how far the tee moves off its original angle. The great amount of variance you see confirms that swinging on plane is a high-precision movement.

I have said that proper swing plane is the result of many sound, proper positions and movements. If you want to play golf in a clear-minded athletic manner, which is how the game should be played, you probably do not want to think intently about swing plane. *In general, checking your plane is a diagnostic measure that a coach or instructor does for you.* However, you can easily work on plane improvement by watching in a mirror at home or by doing drills prescribed by your teacher to help you overcome off-plane swinging automatically.

If you are more comfortable leaving the whole issue of plane to your pro or teacher, you may want to skip the in-depth descriptions that follow.

THE TIPPED-OVER SHAFT

Don't skip on to another chapter without understanding the one Death Move associated with swing plane. I call it the "tipped-over" shaft. When you tip the shaft over in your forward swing, you trap yourself in a position from which there is little or no escape. The shot you hit will almost certainly be a high, weak slice and if not that, a low pull.

Tipping that shaft over on the forward swing (so that the tee in the vent hole points to a line that runs through your toes instead of the line the ball rests on), is truly a Death Move. Very often, the swing that produces this tip over is too flat going back and then too upright (or steep) coming down into the forward swing. The shaft is working in the opposite fashion from a top ball striker.

SUMMARY: BUILDING BLOCKS OF ON-PLANE SWINGING

In the general order of occurrence during the swing, here are the fundamental points of swing plane.

1. There are few, if any, golfers in the world who move the clubshaft/clubhead along exactly the same plane during the backswing and the downswing. The downswing is always narrower than the backswing.

2. Your swing being on plane in the backswing in no way ensures that you will be on plane in the downswing.

3. If you look at the shaft alone, you'll see that most top golfers move up on a plane that is steeper than the plane they come down along. In any case, the downswing plane is more critical than the backswing plane. As noted, the shaft plane flattens on the downswing.

4. In cases in which a player's backswing and forward swing have been coached to move closer to the same plane, the player's accuracy and ball striking generally show a noticeable improvement.

5. There is not a single ideal swing plane that suits all golfers. The amount of individualism in people's swings may prevent that from ever being so. But all players (with the help of a knowledgeable instructor) can understand plane and make critical improvements that bring them closer to the model swing— again, especially on the downward swing of the club. I hope that a careful study of this chapter will allow you to better understand and identify swing plane.

6. The better the ball striker, the better the plane. There truly is a correlation between playing ability and how well a golfer swings on plane. Most low handicappers move the club in a way that is much closer to being on plane than high handicappers.

7. Making swing changes to get the club to move on plane takes hard work and proper practice. Any prompt correction of a

poor plane will take accurate video work, practicing in front of mirrors, and a tremendous number of practice swings. However, if you can consistently get your club on plane in the downswing, you will greatly improve your chances of accurate ball striking.

8. Establishing accurate alignments during the setup is critical to starting the club on plane. Aligning your body in different ways will definitely change your plane tendencies. For example, aim left = shallow plane, aim right = steeper plane. This is a general rule.

9. The right elbow and proper shoulder rotation have much to do with how the club moves on plane. It is most important that the golfer employ the downswing in the correct shift-rotate-hit sequence. As the lower body begins the forward swing, the right elbow and right shoulder will lower and the clubshaft will flatten. This adherence to the laws of human motion corrects many a downswing plane flaw.

10. As I stated, the backswing tends to have two basic planes. Stand behind a skilled golfer. You will see, perhaps to your surprise, that the hands rise up along a curving arc; they do not swing back along Hogan's sheet of glass. If you attempt to swing your hands along that sheet of glass, you will most likely flirt with the Death Move.

11. The slight lateral motion that most great players have in their back swing keeps them on plane without stealing the athletic quality of their swing. Focusing on a steady head (i.e., no movement) often leads to overuse of the arms and lifting the arms over the plane.

12. It is possible to have a perfect swing arc, to be right on plane, yet have either a weak and/or inconsistent swing. This can happen with bad body motion or inconsistent control of the clubface.

13. After impact, the club must swing back to the left. It must not be forced down the target line.

UNDERSTANDING PLANE ANGLE

I have discussed a model swing plane. It is constant and causes a swing that is, in theory, perfect. Now I would like to bring up a subject that is not constant—and is thus a source of much confusion—*plane angle*. Plane angle is the angle between the ground and that part of your body or your equipment that is (or ought to be) moving along a desired flat path. And when I say *desired*, I am taking into account the "situation" of the shot. For example, the plane angle of a nine iron is steeper than the plane angle of a driver and a five iron. Similarly, the plane angle is steeper with the same club when the ball is below the feet than when the ball is above the feet.

RIGHT
The plane angle differs from club to club.

So although the plane is relatively constant for each club and the swing is relatively constant, the plane angle changes from shot to shot, based on the slope of your lie and the club you've selected.

Learning to swing on plane is a requirement for a precision swing that will repeat itself under the pressure of competition. If you follow the fundamentals of human motion and make a true swinging action, you will put your club on plane shot after shot. Clearing up the confusion over plane is an important first step, but practice and frequent lesson checkups (especially with video) are the best ways to develop a solidly on-plane swing.

THE GRIP

Tips and Strategies for Improving Your Hold on the Club

THE JIM McLEAN GRIP PRESSURE SCALE

I developed a 1–10 grip meter scale for my golf schools in the 1980s because I realized that light, medium, and tight were almost useless terms. Light to one student was tight to another. How do you measure medium?

For sure, I can tell you that a tight grip kills your golf swing. Yet for certain shots we need tight grip pressure. So you need to know that a good player actually adjusts grip pressure from shot to shot. Few teachers talk about this. Yet even with perfect technique a mistake in grip pressure can ruin your shot or prevent you from hitting the shot you set up to hit.

Without a doubt, grip pressure is highly underrated. In reality grip pressure is often more important than grip position. This must be true because so many great players position their hands in vastly different configuration. The ultimate key for hand positioning is that the clubface is returned squarely to the ball. A strong grip may work for one player while a weak grip works for another. However, nobody is playing great golf with a tight grip and frozen wrists.

Here are a few things you need to know.

1. Most amateurs grip too tightly.
2. The pressure points (where you feel pressure) are in three locations. The first is the back three fingers of the left hand. Second is the connection between the left thumb and the middle

pocket area of the right hand. Third is the middle two fingers of the right hand.

3. Do not put pressure in the right thumb or the right forefinger (this activates the tendons along the top of the right forearm . . . absolutely where you do not want activation).

4. Form **V**s between the thumb and side of the index finger on both hands. It's a good idea to do this prior to putting the handle of the club into the fingers.

5. A short left thumb shortens your backswing. A long left thumb lengthens your backswing, just the opposite of what most golf books and golf instructors say. A long (extended) left thumb allows more left wrist hinge. Try it yourself.

6. Hold the club up in front of your chest to check your grip. It is much easier to see exactly what your hand position looks like.

GRIP PRESSURE TEST

To check your grip pressure, first be aware of those pressure points.

Now hold a golf club vertical, directly in front of your face. Check your grip position. Adjust the feel in your fingers until you sense that the club is held absolutely as lightly as you can possibly hold it. In other words, the club can almost fall down. Label this as 1 on the grip scale. Then slightly increase the pressure throughout both hands to 2. Work your way up to a mid pressure point of 5. Sense this precisely. From here work up to the tightest pressure possible. This would be 10 on your scale. With practice, you will easily sense ten distinct pressure levels. This exercise will heighten your awareness of pressure and grip feel.

Soon you will be able to sense different levels of pressure in each hand, which will greatly help you hook or slice shots. You will also sense grip level changes throughout the swing. A few examples of how this scale helps my students:

1.   Play normal shots at 5 or under. 4 is a good number for most golfers.

2.   Hold the club tighter for shots around the green, 6 on the scale (chips and pitches).

3.   For putting, most golfers do better at 2, 3, or 4.

4.   Bunker shots around 2.

5.   For long shots out of deep rough, increase grip strength to 7 or 8 to avoid twisting.

THE GRIP

McLean Tips

Develop a grip that gets your clubface square at impact. The grip is not a fundamental, rather it is a connection from the golfer to the club. Slight modifications are required from golfer to golfer.

Understand Grip Pressure. Tension kills the golf swing. On the 1–10 scale I developed for our schools, stay at 5 or less. 1 = superlight, 10 = supertight.

Pressure points:

1.   Unify your grip by closing your right hand over the left. When you do this, the center, or lifeline pocket of your right hand, should fit over your left thumb perfectly. This is a pressure point (or connection point). Do not lose their connection or change your pressure.

2.   Back three fingers of left hand. This activates the tendons under the left forearm. Do not press down with the left forefinger.

3.   Middle two fingers of the right hand. Minimal pressure in the right forefinger and right thumb. Very important.

An interlock or overlapping position is preferred. This unifies your hands. I like the concept of "one giant hand." When you overlap, I like to see the pinkie of your lower hand fit in between the forefinger and middle finger of the hand on top of the handle. With this said, there have been fantastic players with various types of grips, including ten-finger and crosshand.

A company I've worked with (Sports Sense) proved that most amateurs increase their grip pressure by 25 percent or more during the first half of the backswing motion. Therefore, be very careful not to tighten up as you begin the backswing.

When overlapping the little finger of the right hand, do what Ben Hogan advocated in his writing. Press the right pinkie finger down into the knuckle of the left forefinger. This helps unify the grip and helps keep your grip solid at the top.

Have the distinct "feel" that you maintain constant grip pressure throughout the swing.

PREPARATION AND PRESHOT ROUTINE

A Good Setup Procedure Will Help You Produce a Good Shot

To the tour professional, a shot routine that begins the second he or she identifies the ball and starts analyzing the lie and ends with the swing is an essential part of the game that is taken very seriously. The professional knows that all the detailed preparatory work relative to planning a shot has a direct influence on the result. If the golfer goes through a very thorough process of surveying the on-course situation and also visualizes or feels a good shot vividly before swinging, there's an excellent chance that he or she will hit that good shot and be putting for a birdie.

In the case of the typical amateur, most shots are missed before they are played. Why? Due to passiveness or neglect (or ignorance), the average golfer fails to do carefully such vital things as assess the lie, survey the target area, identify the target line, and practice or visualize the swing he or she intends to make when it comes time to hit the ball. The golfer eventually "sets up for failure." Don't make the same mistakes. Instead, adhere to a set shot procedure and "setup for success."

The following routine is not complex, but it is thorough. It is used for every shot and encompasses only that brief period (fifteen to forty-five seconds) during which you are preparing for and executing the shot. For the remainder of the time between shots, relax and have fun with the people in your group. If you make the effort to practice the preshot routine sequence until it is ingrained, you *will* see improvement in your play.

PREPARATION FOR THE ROUTINE

PROCEDURE ONE: SURVEY

A golf course is a diverse environment full of subtleties and surprises. Whether you generally strike the ball seventy times or one hundred times per round, you should devote serious attention to circumstances surrounding your ball—including the lie, distances, and conditions—and the results you want to achieve. Good players notice everything. They don't miss a thing, taking in all pertinent information. The best way to analyze all the variables is to break them down individually, as follows.

LEFT
An uneven lie will change your setup positions and body angles.

RIGHT
Assess all information; here checking wind direction.

LEFT

In preparing to swing, take an extra second to check for "exit" areas near the green.

RIGHT

When hitting to a blind green, it's particularly important to pick a target along the line to the hole, such as a tree in the distance.

A   *Identify Your Ball.*   Make sure the ball you're getting ready to hit is yours. If you hit the wrong ball in a match-play event, you automatically lose the hole. If you hit the wrong ball (except in a hazard) during a stroke-play event, you will be penalized two strokes. Smart players personalize their ball before playing, by putting a mark (e.g., an *X* or three dots) on it with a pencil or pen. The reason: there are many balls with the same brand name and number.

B   *Analyze the Lie.*   Look at the slope of the land, examine the type of grass you're hitting from and the direction it grows, determine if the grass is wet or dry, determine

whether there is hardpan underneath the ball, and so on. An experienced player makes judgments like these in an instant.

C   *Check Your Surroundings.*   Determine whether the stance you'll take will affect any of your positions at address.

D   *Check Wind Direction and Wind Speed.*   Although you should determine the direction of the prevailing wind before teeing off, be careful to not be fooled by flags on greens that are still. They may be blocked by tall trees. Look at the tops of the trees to see if there is wind that will affect your shot.

E   *Identify Your Target Line.*   Identifying the target line will allow you to set properly all of your body alignments. Many golfers choose an intermediate target from one foot to several yards ahead of their ball, on the target line.

F   *Survey the Target Area.*   Is the target area flat, sloping, hard, or soft? Check for your "exit area"—the spot where you'd prefer a poorly hit shot to land. Generally, though not always, one side of the green is more clear of trouble or severe slopes. There are many course situations that call for a more safe play, even for the fine player. For instance, Jack Nicklaus plays to the center of many greens and always clearly analyzes the surrounding safe spots.

G   *Determine Distance.*   The tournament player must be exact and not estimate, must always be aware of the distance to the front edge of the green, and must "carry" yardage over bunkers or water. Such a golfer also must be aware of the depth of the green (front to back) and know the distances to different levels or severe slopes in the green.

RIGHT
A yardage pad or booklet will help
you hit shots the correct distance.

PROCEDURE TWO: VISUALIZE

In your mind, picture the ball leaving and taking a specific trajectory to the target area. If you have any difficulty seeing the shot, simply ask yourself, "What am I trying to do?" Clarity is essential at this point. You must make a pure commitment to your target and have a precise idea of what type of shot you are planning to play.

Form a mental image of the swing. For some folks, this will be detailed and clear. For others, it will be automatic and sensed via "feel."

Dr. Richard Coop, with whom I have conducted some golf schools, has convinced many of the top players in the world that their preshot routine can start with a conscious cue. This cue is your signal to focus on the situation at hand. For the next twenty to thirty seconds, your concentration and visualization are turned on. Some, but certainly not all, golfers benefit greatly by using a conscious cue. Your cue should be some physical act. Golfers who have difficulty with the preshot routine may be helped greatly by using a conscious act or even an audible sound. Here are some examples:

A   Release then reclose the Velcro closure on your glove—this provides an act and a sound together.

B   Tug outward on your shirt and release; do this twice rapidly to produce an act and a sound together.

C   Remove and replace your cap—no sound with this cue.

Be sure to change your cue periodically. You want your cue to be a conscious act, not an unconscious habit. It is done to get you into the "ignition" mode. It causes you to say, "I am going to focus on this shot completely for the next twenty seconds."

BELOW

A conscious cue, such as releasing the Velcro on your glove (left), tugging on your shirt (center), or removing your cap (right), can be used to trigger intense concentration prior to the preshot routine.

Procedure Three: Relax

Stand to the rear of the ball and take a cleansing breath. Exhale twice as slowly as you inhaled. You may want to shake your arms and fingers a bit if you feel extra tension. Use these simple ideas or any other relaxation techniques to get yourself prepared to play. But remember, a relaxed body and a quiet mind are the keys to *peak* performance. Also, it is very possible to be nervous, yet physically relaxed.

RIGHT
Promote relaxation by standing behind the ball and breathing extra slowly. This begins your approach to the setup position.

Procedure Four: Process Your Data

Based on the data, make the club selection that will give you the results you desire.

It's important *not* to choose a club until you have produced a very vivid mental picture of the shot you intend to hit. While on this subject, let me make sure to say this clearly: *don't overdo this procedure*. You can make all of this preshot routine too detailed and overimportant.

When I played on the golf team at the University of Houston, our coach, Dave Williams (seventeen NCAA championships), would become livid if one of his players made too much of the preswing analysis. When a player used the excuse of poor yardage and/or incomplete preparation, Coach would scream, "If you can play this game, you can pick any club. Just take out any club and hit the ball at the flagstick! But don't make excuses and don't be indecisive. And don't ever *look* indecisive." At first glance, this advice may seem farfetched, but believe me, there is truth in those words. *If you can play, you'll be decisive. Your preshot routine will be clear. Too much thinking is just as bad as no thinking—in fact, sometimes much worse.*

THE ROUTINE

1. Make a smooth and graceful walk to the side of the ball. Generally set your alignments and take an effortless practice swing.

Most top players just use a practice motion to release tension and prep themselves. You may want to make the practice swing that is an exact duplicate of the swing you intend to put on the ball. Some players will find this useful. I especially like this procedure for shots around the green.

Good club selection means knowing your game.

2. Approach the ball with your eyes looking at the target. Hold the club in the right hand, step into the "golfer's box" with your right foot, and set the club behind the ball. This procedure, used by many great players, is the most natural and most logical because it ensures that you are "open," which gives you a better visual perspective of the target.

3. After setting the club down, move your feet and body into their correct alignment positions. Take the stance necessary for this particular shot.

Next, look intently at the target, then glance at the ball, while still jockeying your feet for balance. Repeat the look-glance procedure, then go! I say, "Look to the target once, look to the target twice, set, and go"—a proven procedure I stole from the great

Johnny Revolta. Watch and see how many top pro golfers instinc-tively use this simple preshot routine.

The total time for the routine is less than thirty seconds. However, the only segment that truly needs to be precise is after you actually place the clubhead behind the ball and then move your feet into their correct position. That is when I start the stopwatch. Total time for the true routine is only ten seconds or less.

Good players stare at the target and stay in motion. High handicappers do just the opposite. They stare at the ball and have no motion in the lower body. The ball is the most important thing in the world to the poor player. This mistake will cause ten-sion and will result in poor tempo and a vast array of mishits. Don't make this mistake.

REVIEW

To the proficient pro, the preshot routine is *automatic*. However, by writing out all of these minute details, I run the risk of making this process appear tedious and perhaps overimportant to you amateurs. The fact is, you can have the greatest routine in the game but never reach your potential as a golfer if your swing technique is incorrect. With no golf game, a preshot routine is worthless.

GOLFSPEAK: FINAL THOUGHTS ON PREPARATORY MOVES

BODY LANGUAGE

Something very few people consider is body language on the golf course. Yet positive body language is so very obvious with all top players.

I spend a lot of time with my players on this aspect of the game. It's very simple. Look like you know what you are doing! Look and act confident and you will be amazed at the resulting inner confidence in your game.

Anyone who looks scared or looks like they don't belong will usually perform poorly. From spending time with champions, I know they have a special presence. They act, talk, and walk confidently, and take up what I call a lot of "space."

When I played tour events I took up minimum space. I was not comfortable. My body language was poor. I was getting out of everybody's way. I didn't want to be on the stage. In amateur golf I was totally different, but when I stepped onto the tour I didn't carry over the same attitude or the same confident step. How much did that hurt me and how much does it matter to you? Certainly this is an individual situation. However, I do know that you must have confidence in your ability. The way you move gives off a distinct impression to everyone around you. I believe all of what is around you comes back to you. Self-doubt, lack of belief, and noncommitment all show up in your facial expressions and your body actions.

A champion has a certain way about their moves and reactions to any and all situations. I'm saying to you body language is important and I believe hugely underrated. Walk, talk, and act like a champion and over a period of time this will have a positive effect in everything you do in golf.

THE FUNDAMENTALS OF GOLF

Jim McLean's Twenty Fundamentals for Great Ball Striking

These are the fundamentals we teach at our schools. I certainly realize that other teachers and other schools have different fundamentals. If you think about it, who has actually laid out the true fundamentals? Well, I'm going to lay out a list for you to contemplate. In the next chapter I'll present antifundamentals, or misconceptions.

The following are solid fundamentals I've arrived at after a tremendous amount of research. A fundamental is something that all great ball strikers have in common.

McLEAN'S 20 FUNDAMENTALS FOR GREAT BALL STRIKING

1. Center contact. Top players consistently hit the sweet spot.

2. In all great ball strikers the downswing arc is narrower than the backswing arc.

3. There is lateral motion. The hips shift just slightly in the back and around move; however, going forward there is a visible lateral shift.

4. A two-pivot-point swing. Both legs hit the ground and we use both of them. We coil into the back leg and hit off the front leg. This shifting action creates a U-shaped flat spot at the bottom of the swing arc. Weight shift also allows the clubhead to stay closer to the target line for a longer period of time.

5. There are four main power sources: hands, arms, weight shift, and rotation.

6.	The head moves. It goes where the body takes it. The head either rotates or shifts laterally or does a combination of both, in the backswing. After impact the eyes and head rotate forward to catch the flight of the ball and to maintain a powerful and natural swing action.

7.	When the hands get to waist height, the right arm (in the right hander) is even or above the left.

8.	The shoulders out turn the hips in the backswing. I wrote about this in *The X Factor*, which first appeared as a cover story for *Golf* magazine in 1992 and later as a videotape and a book, which focused exclusively on proper body action.

9.	There is some tilt of the upper body toward the ball even at the finish. You do not finish straight up and down.

10.	The hipline rises through impact and to the finish. Your hipline is higher at the finish than it was at impact.

11.	Everything at address (setup) is different at impact. The old idea was to turn and return to the same position or to set up by simulating impact. Both of these are fallacies.

12.	The upper part of the forward arm is connected to the body during and past impact.

13.	The shoulders, upper center, arms, and club rotate in unison past impact through Step Seven.

14.	The left (or forward) wrist is flat or slightly bowed at impact.

15.	The right heel (the back heel) leads the toe of the right foot at impact.

16.	Your upper center is more forward at impact than it was at address.

17.	At impact the hips are more open to the target than your shoulders.

18.	With a driver your head is well behind the ball at impact.

19.	Clubhead speed: all great ball strikers have excellent swing speed.

20.	Halfway down in Step Five, the right elbow leads the right hand.

THE ANTIFUNDAMENTALS OF GOLF

Twenty-five Misconceptions of the Golf Swing

The following are twenty-five misconceptions and nonfundamentals that many golfers still hold on to. There are even many instructors teaching one or more of these misconceptions as true fundamentals of the game, a huge mistake. Incorporating any of these ideas into your swing can ruin you over an extended period of time.

1. Your head is a stationary post. *No.* Your head moves.

2. Stay in your spine angle from start to finish. *No.* All good players stand up somewhat.

3. Your left heel must not rise off the ground in the backswing. *No.* Many PGA Tour players lift their heel in the backswing. Also included in the raise the heel camp were Nicklaus, Snead, Hogan, Jones, Irwin, Miller, and Watson.

4. Swing in a barrel. *No.* Your hips do not turn in a perfect circle.

5. Set up parallel to the target line. *No.* Lots of great players set up off the line both left and right. Most set up left.

6. Keep your feet in place or your back foot should not slide. *No.* Tell that to Davis Love, Nicklaus, Couples, Hogan, Littler, Norman, Casper, and Miller. In fact, you would probably be better off learning to slide the back foot, rather than just going up onto the right toe and keeping the backfoot in place.

7. Set your wrists at a ninety-degree angle when the left arm is parallel to the ground. *Beyond ridiculous.* It leaves out Nicklaus, Woods, Norman . . . to name just a few.

8. Keep your left arm straight. *No.* Less than 5 percent of the entire PGA Tour keeps the left arm straight in a driver swing.

9. Fold your right elbow against your right side in the take-away. *A very old wives' tale.* Nobody does this.

10. Start with your hands ahead of the ball. *On the contrary,* hand position and shaft angle vary from shot to shot. Most great drives actually have the hands behind the ball.

11. Address and impact are similar. *They're not even close.*

12. Grip position must be a certain way. *No way.* The grip is only a connection of the golfer to the club. A great grip returns the clubface to square at impact. That means it can be different from player to player.

13. Golf is a left-sided game. *On the contrary,* many great ball strikers are very right-side dominant: Venturi, Peete, Sutton, Hogan, Leonard. . . . Use your dominant side.

14. The hands and arms supply most of the power. *Okay, try this* . . . sit with your feet off the ground, no shoulder turn allowed, and tell me how far you hit it.

15. There is a perfect position at the top. *No.* As Jackie Burke once asked me, "How stupid are you?" Take the top five money winners each year for the last century and you'll see five different positions at the top.

16. Take the club straight off the ball and swing down the line. *No.* What really should happen is the club swings in a circle around the body. Therefore, you attack the ball from the inside to hit it straight.

17. Keep your head down. *No.* Do this and you guarantee slow swing speeds and an inevitable back injury. You're practicing being a nonathlete when you keep your head down.

18. There is one ball position for all clubs. *No.* Golf is played outdoors.

19. Release the club immediately from the top. This advice is okay as long as at one and the same time you make a powerful

shift to the front leg. Unfortunately, most golfers cannot do this. The result is fat or skulled shots. When you hit the ball solid it is high and weak.

20.   Release equals hand action. *No.* Actually, the "release" refers to your entire right side releasing toward the target. The right hand covers the left well after impact. Thinking of release as just hand action is just beginner golf talk.

21.   The right heel must be on the ground at impact. *No.* On the contrary, Woods, Duval, Nicklaus, and just about all other top players have air under the right heel at impact for full shots.

22.   The clubface must be toe up halfway back. *No.*

23.   You must swing inside-out. This a concept that can greatly help average golfers, but top ball strikers do not swing inside-out. It's an absolute killer for a tournament player. Save your money.

24.   You must be looking at the ball when you hit it. *No.*

25.   If you swing left, the ball will start left. If you swing right, the ball will start on that line to the right. *No.* The fact is the ball will never go where you swing unless the clubface is at a ninety-degree angle to the path.

DEATH MOVES

Extreme Swing Errors That Need Immediate Attention

The following are Death Moves—actions that will kill your game or positions that are so far from ideal that if you do not change your habits, you will hit poor shots forever. With violations of swing fundamentals this dramatic I recommend an immediate change. If you see one of these faults in your golf swing I strongly suggest you go to work immediately. Do not allow one of these swing killers to ruin your ball striking capabilities. If you come to my schools with one of these mistakes, you will definitely be instructed on how to get out of the flaw, and you will leave with ideas on how to eliminate the Death Move.

1.   Freezing over the ball with no waggle and/or ignition movement before moving the club away from the ball. Allowing excessive tension to develop at setup.

2.   Leaving the majority of your weight on your left leg, to such a degree that the left leg becomes the pivot point during the backswing. A classic reverse pivot.

3.   Overextending or disconnecting left arm in the backswing.

4.   Rolling your hands over dramatically in a clockwise direction during the take-away. This rolls the clubface wide open and indicates too much rotation of the left forearm. The club will then be heavy and off balance.

5.   Moving your head toward the target during the backswing. An upper body reverse.

6.   Too little hip turn and/or no weight shift in the back coil.

7. Locking of the right leg in the backswing. (Note I didn't say straightening.)

8. Clubface in an extremely shut position during the backswing and/or at the top of the backswing and/or at step five.

9. Clubface in an extremely open position during the backswing and/or at the top of the backswing and/or at step five.

10. Right arm folding immediately into the body.

11. Clubshaft tip over. This means the clubshaft tips forward in a steep orientation on the downswing. Many amateurs make this absolutely killer mistake. If you see your clubshaft in a vertical position as you start down, it will explain why you almost never hit good golf shots. Few instructors realize just how devastating this move actually is.

12. Clubshaft drops under the right arm as you start the downswing. The clubhead is too far behind you and will approach on too shallow of an attack of the golf ball. You will hit thin or fat shots, plus you will push or badly hook solidly hit shots.

13. The body slides or drifts too far past the ball on the forward swing.

14. Dramatic lifting or dipping in the backswing. This means losing your framework from setup.

15. Weight on toes at setup. Also, during the backswing, the weight must not shift to the toe of the back foot.

16. A fast move away from the ball (hands and club move away from ball without the body). This classic mistake happens to golfers who dominate the swing with the arms and hands. It is a fake turn and a powerless move.

17. Head in front of the ball (driving). No top player ever slides the head past the ball with a driver swing. Check to see how far back your head is at impact. A good rule of thumb is six to ten inches behind the ball.

18. Spin out/No shift. This is the move of a golfer who does not move forward with the lower body. Instead the golfer sits on

the back leg and spins. The result is the upper body opens up too fast, the shoulders are too open, and may have caught up with or even passed the hips.

19.   Throwing the club (narrow to wide) from the top of the backswing. This is a downswing that is initiated by the hands.

20.   Left wrist breakdown at impact. This could be the number one Death Move. Hit tons of smaller shots to break this killer habit.

21.   Left heel backup as the downswing begins. The forward heel actually backs away from the target. Starting down to impact I do not let my students make this move . . . EVER.

22.   Upper left arm disconnection from the left side of the chest. To me the most important connection in golf is the upper left arm to the upper part of the chest through the impact zone. Many golfers break down here. The left elbow breaks down, or the arm saws across the body, or the left arm overextends off the body. Each mistake must be corrected. Again, I don't allow this mistake in my students.

JUNIOR GOLF

Tips for Helping Your Kids with Their Swing

I have been a big proponent of junior golfers for many years, starting with a huge program I helped run at Westchester Country Club in New York. Over these years I believe I've learned some useful information you might relay to your children. At our schools, with junior golfers, mostly we do not identify the steps, even though we are teaching them steps or positions, especially when they are little. I might label the positions with common terms like halfway back or take-away, or top of the backswing, or full finish, simple terms that the children can understand.

If the golf clubs are fit for children, and if they have a good model to watch or someone who swings the club well, children can usually imitate the correct moves very quickly. They do not need a great deal of explanations as adults do. They just need to see what to do and be shown a few additional times in a slower fashion. Our instructors often help the juniors by stepping in and giving them the feel of a good backswing. They may take the club away with the child. Kids generally do not hold the club too tight, so it is pretty easy. It is unusual to see a child with the club gripped firm or tight. However, there is a natural tendency for kids to overswing the club because it is big for them, and they do let the club go anyway because they do things with abandon (a wonderful word for allowing a true swinging action). When we are young we are more likely to have a fearless swing. It is a risk-free type of attitude.

These qualities greatly improve their chances for solid contact and good ball flight. The more swing I see, the better. A true swing will go on a great arc because the club is actually seeking to swing on plane. This is again something that I would never say to a kid. We do not talk about plane and plane angles. Instead we try to get them to have a pleasing and good-looking swing action and to hit the ball with effortless power. It is wonderful to see tapes of kids who have not been overtaught by their parents. You see great stuff. I have been constantly amazed, since I first began to see it using a sequence camera, how great most kids look with very little teaching.

The main thing for juniors to learn is actually the short game; a lot of chipping, pitching, that type of instruction. When they are very small, between three and six, it is just fun, let them do what they can. I would suggest all types of games to teach touch and feel. Between seven and nine, some children get more instruction. You have to be careful at this age. For most of the kids you need to keep it extra simple. One of the primary ways to learn an action is by copying (monkey see monkey do), and kids are great at it. The fewer words we can use and the less verbal teaching we can do, the happier I am with kids. You will find that some children need a lot more help doing things than others. I think I learned more about this when I coached Little League baseball for five years. I found out that a basic throwing action was not automatic to every child and that some needed to be taught. Yet learning young is the greatest way to develop a solid game.

Between ten and twelve, juniors are ready for much more instruction, like building a grip. However, even here there is room for individuality. Carl Welty allowed his younger son, Jason, to play cross-handed. Many kids naturally pick up the club cross-handed. Carl never changed Jason and he is now one of the top amateur players on the West Coast. He is a + 2 handicap and hits it about 320 yards cross-handed. I have seen several other great players use the cross-handed grip, players like Charlie Owens, who was a leading money winner on the senior tour. He is a wonderful player, and there have been others. We do not know what grip is going to work or what position will square the club. Look at Paul Azinger, David Duval, Fred Couples, and Lee Trevino, all with super strong grips. Others have played with weaker grips, like José María Olazabal, Corey Pavin, Johnny Miller, and Bruce Lietzke. Ben Hogan changed to a weak grip after learning with a very strong grip. Generally kids need a stronger grip because it is easier to hit stronger shots and it often places the clubface in a slightly closed position at the top. I personally believe, and I talk to my teachers about it, that a closed clubface at the top is okay, and I like that position. I definitely do not like to see the kids get the clubface open. Tiger Woods played with a closed clubface and won everything as a junior and amateur. Trevino played with a closed clubface. Tom Watson, Tom Weiskopf, Bruce Lietzke, John Mahaffey, Paul Azinger, and so many others are tremendous ball strikers with the closed position at the top of the backswing. So if the kids have it a little closed, I am not opposed, I'll usually leave it alone, which might be unusual for most teachers to say. To my teachers I simply say how do we want the left wrist at impact. The answer is flat or perhaps even slightly bowed. Isn't that what a slightly closed clubface achieves at the backswing position? Something to consider. By the way, I didn't say square at the top is bad. I love it.

Let me finish my comments on juniors by saying position instruction works fantastic at any age. Tiger Woods had his father to model and to teach him classic positions as a young child. Johnny Miller did the same thing with his father by copying positions of Hogan, Snead, and Nelson. Together they would practice great impact positions they saw in photographs. Young Johnny copied the Hogan setup, the Snead finish, and the Nelson leg drive. Later Miller worked with John Geersten, who taught five key positions. I know this because I worked with Mr. Geersten at his club in Monterey myself. Jack Nicklaus began taking lessons with Mr. Jack Grout at age ten. Mr. Grout taught Nicklaus everything, including key positions in the swing.

Do not let anyone tell you that teaching positions is too technical. Done properly and without teaching absolute positions, virtually everybody can improve this way. Juniors, however, generally get these good-looking positions and flowing golf swings much faster than adults. Show them pictures of great players or, like Carl Welty, show them a ton of swings on videotape. You will be surprised how quickly most children come up with a classic-looking style.

You might fairly ask how our schools have done in developing junior golfers. At Doral over the past few years we have had two juniors reach number one ranking in America. Cristie Kerr was actually ranked as both the number one junior and number one women's amateur in America at the same time. Eric Compton reached the number one ranking two years later. James Vargas, from Miami, is currently ranked number two. We have had a USGA junior champion, and many of our juniors from my earliest programs in New York to the present day have gone on to play collegiate golf and even professional golf.

Most important to me is that we teach juniors to love and respect the game of golf. I feel few sports can teach the self-discipline and mental focus required for golf. Our juniors learn the rules of the game and abide by them. They also learn to enjoy golf and to have fun doing it. You cannot force golf or anything else upon a young adult and expect them to stick with it or succeed at it. All I recommend is that you expose your children to the game. Give them the opportunity to see quality golf swings early on. Keep the teaching very simple until the teenage years. Then when you get professional instruction, by all means find a teaching professional who has the skills, desire, and love for teaching junior golfers. That is a formula for developing a lifetime golfer who will love the game.

WOMEN'S GOLF

Swing Actions Especially Designed for Women Golfers

If your instructor charged $1,000 for a single lesson, you would pay it if it were possible to buy a miracle in an hour. Unfortunately, golf is not a matter of miracles, but a game of patience and smart practice. This is especially true for women, who may hold full-time jobs, be full-time mothers, participate in the life of the community, and yet want to play a good game of golf.

There has been much media coverage of the fact that the fastest-growing market for golf is the woman golfer. However, what you don't hear much about is that the highest attrition in golf also occurs among women golfers. Surveys show two primary reasons for the fact that women desert the game of golf faster than men. Frustration from lack of improvement is cited as the first reason. Inability to find quality instruction is cited as the second. These two reasons are closely related, aren't they? If a woman can't find a good instructor, she surely will become frustrated and quit.

Because golf seems difficult at the beginning, it is easy to forget it is a game that is supposed to be fun! For the majority of beginning women golfers, the game is anything but fun. It often ends up becoming an exercise in managed chaos. The game is frustrating and improvement is elusive.

For most people, the early stages of learning golf are difficult. Consistency seems unattainable. Efforts to improve seem futile. But let me tell you what we can do to get you on a program of recovery which will turn it all around.

First, women should know that they do not need to spend hours on the range hitting balls until their hands are sore. Let's be realistic. Women don't have the luxury of those hours to spend in making such a burdensome effort. Effort is not the answer. Mastering of technique is the answer, and proper practice, smart preparation, is the key. In fact, swinging the club in the home for brief periods of time is often better than beating balls on the range. The mirror, in the house, is a great coach.

Women often ask how frequently they should take lessons. The answer depends on the individual's goals, the opportunity to practice and play, and the rate of improvement. I want you to think of your assessment of your improvement in terms of the alphabet. The worst thing you can do for your golf game is take a lesson on D before you are comfortable with ABC. Moreover, you should not pay your instructor to watch you practice ABC. You take your lesson only to validate your progress and teach you new techniques when you are ready. If your instructor won't agree to work with you on reaching realistic goals, one at a time, then find one who will. There is no such thing as the single-lesson miracle, which teaches you the entire game of golf in one hour. There are no shortcuts.

When asking for help, remember that husbands and friends who have been playing longer than you have usually cannot help you improve. They will try to convince you that they can help, but often their advice only adds to the frustration. Everyone who plays golf seems to be a self-appointed expert around others who have played for a shorter time. What you need is a truly certified professional.

When working on the full swing part of the game, keep in mind that you are working on a motor skill. Remember how long it took to get comfortable driving a car or playing a musical instrument and how long before conscious thought was no longer necessary. Remember also that understanding something intellectually does not mean you can execute it physically. To transfer a mental concept of motion into the actual motor skill takes proper practice of the fundamentals, repetition, and time.

Bear in mind, when choosing an instructor, that someone having the title "golf professional" should not necessarily be taken as certification that he or she is qualified to help you. Bear in mind also that finding a professional who plays the game well may not ensure that he or she has teaching skills appropriate to your needs. Ask your prospective instructor pointed questions about his or her qualifications to teach women. You may be surprised at the answers. If the instructor emphasizes the differences in teaching men and women, find another instructor. You want an instructor who simply recognizes that there are subtle differences in teaching women relative to their strength, but not fundamental differences. For example, the beginner woman who is new to athletics needs to feel the use of her wrists and hands more than an athletic male does. Women who are strong and accustomed to athletics can be taught the same positions as any male student. An example of such women players would be an LPGA tour player, a top amateur or junior.

Appreciating the physical differences between men and women has helped me with my teaching. I have come to understand that a woman who has the exact height, weight, size, and age as a man will have one third less muscle mass and smaller hands yet far more flexible hips and shoulders. These components need to be taken into consideration in regard to speed and overall physical strength.

In choosing your instructor, make sure you get a commitment. This commitment is a two-way street. The instructor agrees to a fixed number of lessons over a fixed period of months. The student agrees to a fee and to a certain number of practice hours between lessons.

An equally important alternative to choosing an instructor is consideration of participating in a golf school. In a school, the student will actively work on her game differently than in a private lesson. She will enjoy the power and energy of a group; she will do many drills working on body motion, arm motion, and gaining more speed. At all of our schools, for instance, we work every day on positions necessary to improve each individual's swing. Another major advantage of a school is the fact you do have time to focus on golf. You will be away from home and in a total golf environment.

For women starting the game I break the swing into three positions. We often assign different numbers to my eight steps. For example, we will focus on halfway back, and that becomes number one or letter A, then up to the top of the backswing, number two or letter B, then swing to full, balanced finish, number three or letter C. Although this may seem obvious to the advanced golfer, it is important to know where to swing the club.

Women who participate in one of our golf schools or choose to take private lessons must be aware that the importance of building a perfect swing is overrated. Most of the strokes in a women's game are 65 yards or less. Clearly, the short game for women is all-important! If women are not as strong as men, they cannot hit the ball as far. Therefore, they often are not going to hit as many greens in regulation as they would like. So focusing on the short game is critical. Have you taken lessons and practiced putting, chipping, bunker shots, just to get the ball onto the green in short distances? Probably not. But you should.

Whatever your choice of instruction or practice may be, you must set your own personal par. Regardless of what the scorecard says, your stage of play may mean par is really 6 on a par 3, 8 on a par 4, 10 on a par 5. Imagine how excited you will be if you make your personal par or even a personal birdie on a hole! You are not an expert golfer at the beginning, so don't let the standards set by experts frustrate your personal enjoyment of the game.

In fact, golf can be an easy game to play. Just keep swinging at the ball until it goes into the hole. Golf gets difficult only when you start trying to reduce the number of swings it takes to get the ball in the hole. View that difficulty as a challenge that is made endlessly interesting by the fact that on the course you will never have the exact same shot twice. There will always be some variation—a change in wind speed and direction, the cut of the green, the improvement in your game, the experience of your day-to-day life.

Knowing this truth—that golf is endlessly challenging and variable—I have devoted countless hours studying the swing, the game, and techniques. I have studied how we learn, how our bodies move, and how we improve athletically. Learning to recognize the slight differences necessary to teach women has been a part of that study.

I have found that most women benefit greatly from learning to set the wrist angle sooner rather than later. By that I mean the hands must hinge quite early in the backswing. The angle between the left arm and the clubshaft should form the letter L waist high. Review Step Three and look closely at the photos. Many women grip the club too much in the palm of the left hand (many times because of incorrect grip size) or tighten the wrists in order to stabilize the club at the top. If they grip the club more in the fingers and then learn the proper hinge action, power and improvement will follow.

At our schools we drill this swing action by practicing a pitch shot routine of various lengths every day. We have found that the basic pitch is almost a lost art. Very few people attending a school can execute a proper pitch technique, which does require an early hinge action of the wrists. This wrist set allows you to strike down on the ball with power. The pitch is a shot every woman should learn early. It will benefit every aspect of your full swing technique.

My goal in teaching women has been identical to my goal in teaching men: to make my time with my students a positive learning experience, avoiding temporary cures and short-term results and reducing frustration. I want you to enjoy your lesson and learn to enjoy your golf.

DRIVING GREATNESS
The Art of Driving the Ball with Authority

"If you can't drive the ball, you can't play good golf."

—BEN HOGAN

"The most important club in the bag, in my opinion, is the driver."

—BYRON NELSON

These statements by two of golf's greatest players cannot be ignored.

Although a strong argument can be made that good putting is the most efficient way to lower scores, a reliable driving game seems to be a common denominator of all golf champions. You cannot underestimate the importance of driving the ball well. A successful drive off the first tee sets a positive tone for the entire round, no matter what level player you are. *Jack Nicklaus has even called it the most important shot of the day.* If you can consistently hit the ball far down the fairway, you are a skilled driver with a tremendous competitive advantage. Good driving puts you in an offensive position, whereas weak driving puts you in a defensive position. Think of the intimidation factor Tiger Woods has with his long, straight driving.

This chapter is devoted to the unique requirements and tactics of driving. In no way, however, do I believe there is a separate driver swing. Yet I would like to share some important *setup* adjustments and *mental* adjustments that are unique to the driver swing and can greatly aid your performance off the tee. These ideas correlate with the material in Chapter 4 "The Eight-Step Swing," but they favor some parameters and preferences that were designated "acceptable" in that chapter but that I identify here as being particularly suited to better driving.

Ken Venturi's influence is evident throughout my statements and writings about the golf swing, and his approach to driving impresses me as much today as it did in the mid-1970s. During that period, I played many rounds with Venturi, which is to say, I witnessed a master shot maker one on one. Venturi's ball striking was pure genius. I roomed with Bruce Lietzke, Bill Rogers, and John Mahaffey at the University of Houston, and I have played numerous competitive rounds with Lanny Wadkins, Tom Kite, Ben Crenshaw, Johnny Miller, and others. Although all of them were/are tremendous ball strikers, none of them could maneuver the ball with better precision than Venturi. When I played with him, away from tournament pressure, when putting did not matter, Venturi could still do absolutely anything with the golf ball, on command. Here are the best driving tips he has shared with me.

A   *Use a wide base.* The best drivers place their feet wider than shoulder width apart. Past professionals who were considered premier drivers and who played from a wide base include Ben Hogan and Byron Nelson. Today, Lee Trevino, Arnold Palmer, and Bruce Lietzke depend on the same setup key. The wide base encourages a shallower swing and an elongated "flat spot" through the hitting area, which is ideal for accurate driving. The wide stance provides a low center of gravity for stability and allows a player to "pump" the feet off the ground more powerfully. If you had one chance to deliver your hardest punch and win the heavyweight crown, you would instinctively spread your feet. When a baseball slugger connects with power, it's because he or she has stepped forward and hit from a broad base.

B   *Play the ball off your left heel.* This ball position takes maximum advantage of the flat spot in your sweeping driver swing.

C   *Favor a fade.* Many fine golfers play a fade because they find it to be the ideal control shot in golf. If you're strong and have good hand-eye coordination, try it.

SAME, SAME, SAME

Driving, unlike any other shot in golf, allows you to eliminate most variables. Most every teeing area is dead flat, the grass on the tee is mowed low, you can tee your ball to exactly the same height every time, and you can create the angle you want by teeing up next to the left or right marker, or between them. So what you want to do on the tee is to create the "basketball free throw" mentality. That is, make every drive the same. Change nothing. Go through the same routine every time and play the same drive on every hole. Allow no variables in your thinking or your shot pattern.

RIGHT

Two driving tips emphasized by Ken Venturi were to assume a wide base and to lower your center of gravity.

RIGHT

Two driving tips emphasized by Ken Venturi were to assume a wide base and to lower your center of gravity.

HOW TO FIGHT FIRST-TEE FRIGHT

1. On the driving range before the round, imagine the shot you'll need on the first tee, then aim at a particular area to simulate the first fairway.

2. Select the long club that you play with the most confidence. For many golfers, the 3 wood is the best selection.

3. Approach the ball from behind, focusing hard on your landing area and visualizing a perfect drive hitting it.

4. At address, depend on one swing thought that you know works. Do not freeze over the ball, running through a long checklist of swing keys in your head.

5. Once you feel comfortable, make an uninhibited, tension-free swing. Let go!

One of the great professional drivers of all time is Bruce Lietzke. I lived with Lietzke at the University of Houston (we also roomed together at all away tournaments and, later, on the mini tour), and I'd like to pass on some of my observations.

Lietzke has reduced all his planning and thinking to a bare minimum. Every drive Lietzke hits is the same: he aims down the left side of every fairway. He visualizes the ball *fading* into the center of the landing area. He addresses his ball and trusts his swing. He lets go. Lietzke's "fade control" is the chief reason why he is usually the PGA Tour's best overall driver. This category combines distance and accuracy.

An average putter at best, Lietzke has been a money machine on the tour. What's more, he rarely practices and actually plays fewer events than any tour regular. Supertalented? Yes, but Lietzke also has superior golf smarts. He eliminates the left side of every hole on every golf course he plays. This is especially beneficial in driving, because driving is what sets up good scoring possibilities.

Lietzke's driving game allows him to stay on the *offensive* at all times, especially down the stretch. If you looked up Lietzke's final-round scoring average over his career, you'll see it is one of the best ever. One major reason for his Sunday success is his ability to drive it long and straight.

I hold up Lietzke's driving game as a model for my students to emulate. Especially in your driving, go up there with a plan, a visual picture, and a chosen shot shape. Eliminate every variable you can. Keep your plan and all your thoughts as simple as possible.

Of course, you may naturally ask, "What does Bruce Lietzke do when he comes to a hole that requires a right-to-left tee shot?" The answer is so simple, it's scary: he doesn't hit his driver. As Lietzke says, his driver "is not allowed to know it can hook the ball!"

Along with Lietzke, there have been quite a few other top performers whose driving games have been based on a controlled, powerful fade. Jack Nicklaus, Ben Hogan, Lee Trevino, and Hale Irwin all played the power fade. For aspiring players, this should be food for thought.

A LITTLE HELP FROM MY FRIENDS

A DRIVING TIP FROM AL MENGERT

The first golf lessons I ever took were in Seattle in 1966, from Al Mengert, who had worked under Claude Harmon at

Winged Foot and Tommy Armour in Boca Raton. Mengert showed me that from the tee the fairway was actually a *three-lane highway*.

If you play a draw, you should aim down the right lane and plan to land the ball on the center lane (middle of fairway). If you hit it straight, you end up in the right lane—the right side of the fairway, which is fine. If you hit your planned shot, you are dead center: "Position A." If you hit too much draw, chances are you will still end up in the left lane of the fairway. (Never aim a drive so that a straight ball will go into trouble.) This "driver's education lesson" will allow you to use the *whole fairway* and increase your chances of staying on the short grass.

A DRIVING TIP FROM JACKIE BURKE

When I played on the golf team at the University of Houston, we had the opportunity to play with and learn from Jackie Burke—one of golf's finest thinkers who won both the Masters and PGA Championships. Burke didn't just suggest to us that we "let go with the driver," he preached it nonstop! He found the idea of guiding or steering your drives totally repugnant. "Let go. Give up control. Abandonment." These are the ideas he adhered to in regard to driving. To be great, he told us, "you must have some *recklessness* to your swing."

The best visual image he offered was this: "Imagine you are trying to drive the ball into the Atlantic Ocean. There is no way to miss. You could hit it anywhere. So swing freely." He reasoned that with no interfering thoughts we would find ourselves hitting solid drives virtually on a string.

This single thought has helped me get through some tremendously stressful situations in decent fashion. I highly recommend this *let go* mentality whenever the going gets particularly tough.

CLOSING THOUGHTS ON DRIVING

Some of the best ideas for driving are actually very simple. Stay relaxed and loose for extra control of the ball. For extra distance, tee it high. Maintain your grip pressure from address all the way to finish. Make a balanced swing and sense that the fastest part of your golf swing is past the ball. Visualize your favorite hole or a beautiful flight of your upcoming shot, trust your swing, and let go.

DRILLS TO IMPROVE YOUR DRIVING

1. *Train Your Right Side.* Practice a natural side-arm tossing motion with your right arm. Practice the correct positions in the Eight Steps by swinging a club with your right hand and arm only.

2. *Play Tee-ball Golf.* When you can, play nine holes alone. Hit ten drives off each tee, then go to the next hole. Assuming the nine has two par-three holes, you will be hitting seventy driver shots to actual landing areas of regulation holes. Keep track of the number of fairways you hit.

3. *Drag the Clubhead.* Gardner Dickinson, a legendary player and teacher, devised a drill that helps you swing in such a way that the clubhead approaches the ball on a shallower angle, ensuring solid contact. For good players, this drill produces the feeling of taking the hands out of the swing.

Address an imaginary ball and take your normal stance, but set the clubhead down even with your right foot. Make sure the clubhead is inside the target line and the clubface is open. Now drag the clubhead forward through the imaginary ball, making a conscious effort to close the clubface—to square the toe through impact. On the follow-through, the toe of the clubface should point skyward. Continue through to a full, balanced finish,

RIGHT
*Swinging with your right hand only
will only improve your driving skills.*

extending your right arm while the left arm folds at the elbow. This will give you the sensation of the no-hands release and shallower angle of approach through impact and into the finish position.

4. *Sweep the Ball Drill.* This has been a lifesaver drill I've used for good players who experience a severe driving slump; it teaches many of the fundamentals seen in great drivers. It is performed with a fairway wood that features four or five wood loft, a shallow face, and a smaller-profile clubhead. Because the point of the drill is to pick the ball cleanly off the tee with a sweeping swing, this type of club is ideal. That's because any swings delivered along a steep swing path will produce an extra-high "skied" shot; letting you know instantly that your technique was incorrect.

To do the drill, tee the ball one inch off the ground. Check all your alignments and check your posture as you address the ball.

Unify your hands at address, by establishing a secure grip that still allows mobility in the wrists. Grip slightly tighter in the last three fingers of the left hand, but keep the left arm limp and tension free. Now swing back with what feels like a halfbackswing, at about 60 percent of full force. Because the club and arms never get high in the backswing, you cannot swing along a steep incline.

Initiate the change of direction from backswing to forward swing *from the ground up*. The clubhead will be only about shoulder high in the backswing as you initiate the forward motion. Feel your feet, knees, and hips shift laterally. This lateral movement should occur before the clubhead has completed its backward arc. Once it's triggered, the clubshaft will fall into the slot (i.e., approach the ball from an inside and shallow "attack track"), wrist cock will increase, the right elbow will start down toward the ball, the width of the swing will narrow dramatically from the backswing to the forward swing, and you will sense an *out-in* or *wide-to-narrow action*.

As you swing through the ball fully, make a "no-hands" release and keep your left wrist solid. Allow your left elbow to fold after impact and your right arm to elongate.

If you made no effort to swing with your hands, you'll feel the club sweeping powerfully through the ball, with the clubface staying on the clubface longer at impact. You'll also feel your hands and arms coming up in front of your chest, which is a good sign. It is truly an awesome feeling to experience.

The shot you will hit is a low, line-drive draw; the draw coming not from flipping the hands but instead from "firing" your entire right side. One final point to check on your no hands back-and-through swing: look for the toe of the club to be up on both sides of the swing.

Remember: It's a mini-swing drill with the purpose being to deliver a shallow arc. The small swing done correctly will give you incredible distance—much more than expected.

5. *Hit Drives between Flagpoles.* On the range, pick out a thirty-yard-wide landing area, then hit drives into the gap

between two real or imaginary flagpoles. Keep track of your success rate whenever you do this. I recommend that you hit thirty drives, keeping track of how many fairways you hit.

JIM McLEAN'S TIP SHEET FOR GOOD DRIVING

On the tee, you should

- Use a driver that is esthetically pleasing to the eye and features the correct loft, lie, and shaft flex for *you*.
- Adhere to a confident preshot routine.
- Love the challenge of driving the ball powerfully and accurately.
- Think positively.
- Play a shot.
- Relax your grip pressure when you set up.
- Soften your arms and keep your wrists flexible at address.
- Feel and sense the center of your body initiating the swing.
- Connect your arm swing to the rotation of your body.
- Employ good footwork.
- Stay level during the swing.
- Strive for solid contact and center hits.
- Make your right shoulder, right hip, and right knee finish past the centerline of your body that is first established at address.
- Drive the ball through an imaginary window, positioned ten feet out in front of you, along the target line.

Great drivers

- Visualize the optimum shot. Don't freeze over the ball; stay in motion before pulling the trigger.

- Let go.
- Have two pivot points (the two legs) in their swings.
- Have some lateral motion in their swings.
- Have a shallow angle of attack.
- Have a long flat spot in their swings.
- Hit past the ball.
- Go to a full finish position.
- Have an athletic motion.
- Swing within themselves.
- Have extra power in reserve.

SWING LEFT TO SWING RIGHT

A Novel Approach to Straightening Out Your Swing

I wrote an article way back in the 1980s with the same title as this chapter title. Back then it was a very controversial topic. It seemed to contradict widely held beliefs, dropping the club to the inside, staying under the shot, hitting from the inside out, and swinging for as long as possible down the target line.

My observations of the great ball strikers and researching photos and videotapes indicated that the club swung to the left after impact much faster than most teachers believed. It did not make sense. How could swinging left make the ball go straight? I believe the golf club moves around after impact more than we see. A key fundamental is the swing plane after impact. I also like to have my students keep their arms low and left after impact. A tight pulling left arm prevents this from happening properly. Instead, the left arm must stay in close to the upper left side. The right side and right arm must do their work.

For many people, the effort to swing to a high finish or to stay behind the ball will bring the arms up high early past impact. With this arm action, the shaft tilts to a markedly vertical orientation. Even for the advanced player, this style of release needs explanation. By nature, shots hit from this position are more oblique to the target line and can stray farther left or right than the swing action would seem to indicate. Generally, though, it's a hooking topspin sort of action that is imparted.

The swing thought that will prevent this error is "low arms through impact." I ask my advanced students to keep both arms down past impact and underneath the shoulders all the way to the waist-high position. To do this, keep the horizontal lines of the body more level through the swing. As the downswing begins, the right shoulder drops and begins to rotate forward. Even though you know it will lower, instead think "level." The swing-left-low, arms-on-plane follow-through requires most players to feel a high right side.

Another productive thought can be to pull the left arm and the golf club consciously leftward with center. This is done with a rock-solid left wrist with no breakdown; there is a feeling of the back of the left wrist and the left arm staying with the rotation of the body and *pulling left*. Again, this is a great antihook image, one that has worked well for tour player Bill Britton. It helped him straighten out his shots immensely.

The basic dynamics of this left-sided pulling motion can be encapsulated in the following manner: stand up near a wall, with your right shoulder and right side several feet away, and extend your left arm as if you were about to shake hands using your left hand. Your left arm is bent at the elbow and the palm of your left hand is open. Your left palm will directly face the wall. Make sure you feel a bend in that left elbow and that you feel a strong *connectedness* that comes out of your left shoulder and left pectoral region, extending almost all the way down to the elbow. Now shut your hand fairly tightly as though you have just grasped the end of a chain that you are attempting to pull out of the wall. To pull the chain free you would use your whole body. Your left arm would stay connected to the rotation of the body and you'd jerk that chain out of the wall in a "level left" movement. This has been a tremendous teaching thought for me, which I sometimes

extend to a feeling of the left shoulder staying down through the shot.

THE TWO CORNERS OF THE SWING

When the hands reach their low point in the downswing, the hands should be several feet away from the ball. After impact the hands should stay very level and go left with your lower center. They will hit the forward corner of the swing. Golfers who push the ball, hook, or hit extra high shots typically miss the forward corner of the swing.

Another positive, effective image I have used with accomplished players is the Charlie Sifford swing, in which Sifford swings the arms underneath his trademark cigar. Sifford, of course, was a cigar smoker, and anyone who has seen him play golf would notice a very high right side, a low left side, and a very forward motion going through the ball. Sifford has been one of the great straight-ball hitters and drivers of all time.

I had the opportunity to play with Sifford and found he was also a particularly great wind player. The trajectory of his ball was down, because he moved his body with such a level turn, keyed by his high right side. This is a tremendous way to play golf, because it has the appearance of a "comeover," but it produces a beautiful, straight golf shot. This is the swing feeling that Britton adopted to win the 1989 Centel Classic. He felt as though he were staying under the cigar and going left through the golf shot with a low finish or, you might say, a "high right side."

Yet another swing key you can work on to groove a hookproof swing is to allow your *right arm* to go across your chest as the clubhead moves through the ball. If you do this correctly, your hands will feel as if they were left of your right shoulder through impact, almost in a *crossing motion*. Once again, this tip is for golfers who stay behind the ball too long and swing the club out to the right too much. They have experienced overkill on the *inside-out motion*. I see many lower-handicap players who have worked hard to achieve the inside-out swing and as a result have lost the chance to play really good golf. They are destined to hook the ball the rest of their golfing life unless they can correct their swing path problem.

In working extensively with Tom Kite throughout 1992 when he won the U.S. Open, this hookproof swing-left concept was the single greatest change he made. I believe it increased Kite's accuracy through the bag and definitely helped him drive the ball much farther.

I've used this concept with Cristie Kerr, Greg Kraft, Len Mattiace, Robin Freeman, Peter Jacobsen, Gary Player, Liselotte Neumann, and many other top tour professionals, with great results.

THE RIGHT MINDSET
Confusion Can Open the Door to Discovery

Improving your golf game is a mental, physical—some would say spiritual—quest. It's a wonderful, worthy endeavor, but it comes a lot easier to someone who can handle momentary confusion. You see, in golf, confusion is sometimes *necessary*. Rather than something to avoid, confusion in the learning process is actually something to welcome. Confusion indicates to me that a student is truly thinking or feeling in a new way. If you think of confusion in this manner, it can open your mind.

In plain fact, any time you take a formal lesson from a professional, try a tip from a golf magazine, or attempt to change your golf game in any way, you're likely to become slightly confused. Whatever the change, be it a theory or a drill or an idea, it should result in a new "feel." This change in feel, this departure from your normal technique, is what triggers mental confusion. But confusion can be a good thing and a very normal part of the learning process. In fact, *confusion can actually open the door to discovering new ways to swing and play better golf.*

The best way to handle confusion is to see past it, to the new understanding that awaits you. As you work through changes in your mind (and body), you should welcome feeling new sensations involved in the swing, even though you aren't quite sure where each one will take you. If, in the end, these new elements of change don't feel good or fail to help you swing better, you can always go back to where you were before, knowing at the very least that *you gained by learning what doesn't work for you.*

The alternatives to the improvement quest are giving up completely on new thoughts or, deciding that you are satisfied with where you are. In either case, you stop learning. By quitting, you admit that either you've "got it" or you never had all the answers and that you are satisfied with the golf skills you presently possess. No problem with this, except that I find most golfers are naturally curious and do possess an inner desire to excel. Some people will resist all change, yet we know change is the only thing that brings about progress for someone making fundamental mistakes. Hard work and repetition of the same old wrong techniques is *not* the path to mastery.

The swing is vastly complex, and there are many ways to attain excellent results. There are many paths that can be taken and many that will allow you to reach a satisfactory destination. However, now is a good time to sound a warning: *An abundance of what is written on the golf swing is controversial and contradicts other expert views, point by point. Mixing ideas from totally different concepts can be frustrating and is usually counterproductive.* Without any doubt, there is a ton of misleading advice that I find *fundamentally* incorrect. They may well be teaching things that virtually no top players use. Going down one of these paths will lead to disastrous confusion and worse golf.

An interesting situation arises when a pure "method" teacher meets a student who believes *completely* in the method being taught and is physically adaptable to it. At that point, the golfer becomes a disciple. He or she accepts absolute statements about the golf swing the way zealots accept their religious tenets. The human mind is so strong that total belief in a teacher's method literally makes things happen. Thus the student reaches a high level of mental clarity and focus. If the method is sound, the result: an average golfer becomes good; a good golfer becomes great.

Having said this, I'm truly convinced that the best method in the world cannot suit every golfer or even most golfers. The game and the swing are too individualized to allow for a series of absolutes. As I see it, there can be no unquestionably "correct way" to teach every player. Pure "method instructors" who become confident that they have seen it all and learned it all have probably just stopped noticing new things and have begun looking only for what they want to see. Students who never experience even a moment of confusion are either vastly brilliant or closed-minded.

On the driving range, most of you have experienced that odd feeling of hitting virtually every shot exactly as you want, to the point that you decide to experiment. You ask yourself, "Can I switch to a different swing action or swing thought and still get excellent results?" or "Now that I'm hitting the ball on the exact line as planned, can I stretch out the shot and get better distance?" Often, of course, this questioning process breaks your good swing and shot-making spell, but I wouldn't be too quick to criticize you for being inquisitive. Golf is such a demanding quest, we are often unable to discontinue searching, even when our goals are temporarily reached. We all tend to want just a little bit more. As the great Jackie Burke always schooled me, "golf is a game of upgrading."

Ironically, when you have something that works, it is not a sure indication that this is the only answer. It doesn't mean that another approach will not work or that trying a new approach won't produce better results or a more interesting experience. However, be careful not to become too much of a technical perfectionist, or you'll experiment forever. Seek to *crystallize* your concept of what you are doing, bearing in mind that the key points within that concept will change and develop and, one hopes, improve your game even more.

I tell some of my students it may actually be better for them to accentuate their uniqueness, rather than try to swing like everyone else. Difference is one definition of greatness, is it not? Great athletes all use divergent ideas and techniques to perform

at their peak levels. Consider, for example, the varying techniques of Ben Hogan, Jack Nicklaus, Lee Trevino, Fred Couples, Corey Pavin, Ray Floyd, Lanny Wadkins, John Daly, Bruce Lietzke, and Curtis Strange, Jim Furyk, and Sergio Garcia.

Belief in yourself is the key ingredient to greatness. "Belief is durable" the saying goes, and in golf that means trusting your system, your swing method, and your style of play. It is difficult or impossible to alter a person's deeper beliefs; this is a simple fact. Over time, however, beliefs can change. For example, some of my teenage thoughts about the golf swing now seem ridiculous to me. I remember that when my boys were three and four years old, they believed with all of their hearts that a monster lived in the closet. My point: believing does not, in the end, make something true. But remember, beliefs are very powerful.

Another axiom holds: "It is better to travel hopefully than to arrive." But sometimes we do arrive. If, in your quest, you have used a drill to work toward a certain feeling and result and you get that result, it's time to put aside the drill. Come back to the drill if the fundamentals it has helped you refine begin to break down, but know when to stop.

The bottom line is that only one person can make you great. That person is you, not some teacher. Teachers, books, and methods can provide only limited assistance and guidance. You alone must do the work and pay the price through hard, honest practice. You alone must be able to withstand pressure and hit the shots on the most solitary stage of all—the golf course.

The quest is similar from golfer to golfer, but there are many paths to choose from. *Doing it one's own way (with or without an instructor's help) produces the greatness of champions.* To believe in yourself is to have power; whereas conforming to the current norms will almost always create mediocrity, leaving you just short of your personal best and far short of brilliance. Only you can make the choice as to what physical skills and drills you will use to become a total player. The interesting outcome of it all is that, at a certain advanced stage of play, the game of golf becomes almost totally *mental*.

HOW TO PREPARE

Establishing a Good Battle Plan Is Bound to Raise Your Level of Play in Tournaments

Golfers who like to compete do not like to approach a tournament without being fully prepared. But, honestly, what percentage of the time can you expect to bring your A game into competition? Usually there is some facet, maybe your driver, your putter, or your short-iron game, that is not at its sharpest.

If that's the bad news, then the good news is this: no matter how well or poorly you are playing, no matter what your realistic chances are of winning the tournament, you can *always* win what I call the "four battles." By being totally prepared in these four areas, you will be at your best for any important event you enter.

Credit for this proven concept of establishing a competitive golf "battle plan" goes to Coach Jim Young and the Performance Institute of the Academy at West Point. He told me that there were five contests within every game that his Army varsity football team could win. Let me explain. The Army team applied a basic game plan to each contest it played. The idea was that even if Army was playing number-one-ranked Notre Dame the team could still win individual aspects of the game, which could, in the end, lead to victory or at least a highly competitive game. I wondered if I could apply this same thinking to golf. Eventually, I came up with the following four-point battle plan, designed to help you perform more proficiently under pressure.

BATTLE NUMBER ONE

WIN the Pretournament Battle.   To win the pretournament battle, you must begin your preparation for the tournament well in advance. Finish up projects that have been hanging. Get to all those long, important phone calls to business associates and family. Go to the eye doctor, the dentist, the chiropractor. Then begin your homework on the golf course you'll be playing. Even if you've played it many times, walk it with a notepad and pencil. Determine where you want to hit the ball, then locate the "bailout" spots where you wouldn't mind seeing your mishit shots land. Where there's a layup shot facing you, plan that layup shot down to the last little bounce, making sure to land the ball a specific distance from the pin. Be sure you know exactly how far you are hitting your wedges that day. Finally, carefully analyze your golf game. Determine what area of your game needs the most work and get to it. (Always spend some extra time before any event working on putting and chipping.) The object is to begin all your tournament preparations well in advance.

BATTLE NUMBER TWO

WIN the Preround Battle.   Start by getting your equipment in perfect order. Make sure every grip is clean and tacky; every groove on every iron is scraped clean; your golf balls are marked for identification; your shoes are respiked; and you've got extra gloves, sweater, sunscreen, lip balm, water jug, lucky socks, and whatever you could possibly think of later so you don't say, "I wish I'd brought my . . ."

Then, every day of the event, block out an excessively long space of time between your departure for the course and your tee time. Know exactly how long it takes to get to the golf course and then give yourself twice that amount of time. I remember the first time I saw Lee Trevino in the locker room at Sleepy Hollow Country Club, in Scarborough, New York, several hours before his tee time for the PGA Senior Tour Commemorative. I asked him why he was so early, and he explained to me his routine—the point of which is to leave nothing to chance and to remove completely the possibility of feeling rushed. If Trevino hits traffic, needs gas, has a flat tire, takes a wrong turn, he never has to worry, because he factors these long-shot possibilities into his schedule. Trevino can always be found in the locker room well before his scheduled tee time in a tournament, doing what some people would call wasting time. True, he is talking, resting, or just hanging out—but he's not wasting time. He's preparing to win a golf tournament, and he knows that to play his best he has to have some down time among all the essentials of travel, getting dressed, eating, and hitting practice shots. By arriving extra early, Lee knows he will walk out of that locker room for his pre-round practice exactly on time. He will be ready to focus and he will never be rushed.

You *can't* control how the wind blows, so concentrate on the things you can control, one of which is remembering to check the wind direction before teeing off and to anticipate how and which way it will be blowing on every hole. Usually, there is a flag near the clubhouse that will help this determination. Remember that on the course the wind may be swirling through different areas and can fool you if you are not truly aware of the general direction.

Go through your warmup routine in exactly the way it makes you feel most comfortable. I recommend putting first and then going to the driving range to warm up the full swing. I feel that those warmup putts are quite important (especially some long lag putts) to establish the green speed and your "feel" for the day.

Finish your warm-up session using the club you will hit off the first tee. Rehearse that shot in detail and you will feel much more relaxed heading to the first tee. Allow extra time to reach

the tee. This will allow you to focus and prepare for your all-important first tee shot of the day.

BATTLE NUMBER THREE

WIN the Emotional Battle.   Entire books are written about the emotional and mental approach to sports, including golf. You should know the mental/emotional state that allows you to perform at your best. The one tip I would add is this: before you tee off, it is often helpful to realize that every round usually has bogeys in it. The thing is, we don't know where, when, or if they will come. Many fine rounds have early bogeys, sometimes two in a row. Promise yourself that if you bogey hole one and hole two,

FOCUS ON YOUR PERFORMANCE!

$$\frac{P}{R} = \$$$

$$\frac{R}{P} = 0$$

you will visualize your scorecard with those bogeys isolated among a long string of pars. Remember that scoring bogeys on holes number one and two is not a sure sign of your worst round. On the other hand, if you start out with two birdies, the reverse is true. It does not mean you should do anything different. Stick to your game plan and do not project results. Continue your shot-by-shot mentality. Stay in the present tense. Accept your success without taking on any doubts or unreal responsibilities to shoot a record score.

Winning the emotional battle will be more difficult on certain days. However, this remains a battle that you are capable of winning every time, provided you maintain your composure, even when you swing poorly or don't score to the best of your abilities on a particular hole or several holes.

Anger usually brings mistakes that add strokes to your score. Needless risks are then taken, and your score gets worse. That is why it's extremely important to stay mentally level and focused. Sure, I know it's easy to get upset in golf. The irony is, in some cases that anger can be helpful in snapping you out of a funk. However, if you go into each round knowing that luck is involved and that every shot you hit will not be your best, then attitude problems can be greatly reduced.

I find it very useful to have students keep things in perspective. We would all do well to play golf shot by shot or hole by hole, and leave each hole behind as we move to the next. So many of us play golf in the past or in the future, when we really need to play in the present.

Jackie Burke always told the University of Houston golf team to focus on the performance at hand and to forget about results. Burke taught me a number of vital lessons about golf during my college days, but none was more important than his two-sided formula of $P/R = \$$, whereas $R/P = 0$. Translation: *performance over results leads to success, whereas emphasizing results over performance leads to failure.*

It's okay to form a result-oriented goal. But if you are result conscious while you are performing, if you think ahead while there are shots still to be hit, you may not be able to take care of the shot at hand. Your mind will be distracted from the present and your performance will not be 100 percent. Living in the future or the past is not the optimal performance state. It is a distraction. Take care of the shot at hand and those coveted good results will happen. *Performance first—always.*

BATTLE NUMBER FOUR

WIN the Management Battle.   Before you tee off, eat and drink what you need to avoid mental or physical fatigue. Then once you begin your round, you will stay mentally connected to the golf course and how it's playing, especially in regard to wind, moisture, dryness, mowing, watering, etc. Promise yourself that you won't get caught on a tee without the right club, because you let the caddie walk ahead or you parked the cart too far away. Promise yourself that you will follow a set "game plan" that involves not taking unrealistic risks. Between shots, relax and pace yourself. Do not try to concentrate intensely for the full duration of the round.

Winning the management battle requires that you fairly assess your strengths and weaknesses and then maximize your strengths. Good course managers do not make dumb mistakes. They are aware of everything and miss nothing. They can "zone out" distractions. They plan and "see" each shot. Currently Tiger Woods displays perfect management skills and is a great model.

Golf is a game of adjustments, and usually the player who makes the fewest and the least-costly mistakes will remain in the game with a good chance to win. Whatever physical mistakes you commit in competition, you should be able to contain them and move on if your preparation is thorough and if you make sure to control everything that's controllable.

I believe that it's possible for you to win all four of these battles. Try, and you will give yourself the best opportunity to compete at your optimum level, time and time again.

How many golfers do you know whose swings are far short of classic? Who don't get much distance on their drives? Who play a slice with every club but the short irons? And who, despite these shortcomings, post impressive scores and often win the "Nassau bet"? These are the golfers who know themselves and know their games, who play within themselves and are good course managers. As John Wooden (the wizard of UCLA) once said, "Don't let what you cannot do interfere with what you can do."

To make sure we distribute the satisfaction these golfers feel more widely among the population, teachers must begin emphasizing course management so that students understand that management skills depend on how well they know themselves and their game and how well they translate this knowledge into a sound plan by which to play each hole.

When sports psychology experts like Dick Coop, Bob Rotella, Fran Pirozzolo, and Chuck Hogan discuss the mental side of golf, they never stray far from the principle of *self-knowledge*. Of all games, golf exposes fraud and self-delusion most efficiently. There is no other sport besides perhaps the high jump or pole vault in which, before we play, it is so obvious what we are trying to do. In effect, we golfers call our shots every time we come to bat. If we can point to the center field bleachers (by selecting our 3 wood trying to reach a lakeside par five from 240 yards), then hit the ball there, hurrah for us. Likewise, if we can plan the golf equivalent of a walk, a hit-and-run single, and a squeeze bunt, and still make birdie, we've succeeded just as well. If you are not in touch with your own ability and your own golf psyche, your competitors will know soon enough that—whatever kind of player you are—you've got a lousy manager in *your* dugout.

In the past few years, CBS's Gary McCord and other TV golf announcers have described many a successful golf shot by calling it a "good play." This phrase has always been appropriate to sports in which the athlete must react to a situation, such as when a shortstop charges a slow roller and throws home or a point guard hits the open player underneath for a layup. But in golf, with a ball and a target that don't move, does it make sense to say, "good play"? The answer is yes, absolutely. The key is not whether things are moving or standing still, it's whether or not there are options and choices. Like the shortstop and the point guard, the golfer has options. He or she has more time to think but also has a greater number of options, on most shots. When tour players assess the lie, the competition's standing, the score they need to make, and the strengths and weaknesses of their game, they are reacting to a situation. If they read the situation improperly, they can hit what you'd have to call a good shot and still be in trouble. When they devise a plan—from club selection, to swing technique, to the shape of the shot—and go on to execute it, the two words they are truly hoping to hear from the caddie are *good play*.

Most of us make good plays when we are at peace with ourselves and feel an inward calm. Here are two proven ways to achieve a golf state of mind that will enhance your performance.

- *Assess the game you've brought to the course that day.* Once you take an honest account of the current state of your golf skills, you are ready to establish a game plan based on shots you are comfortable executing, as opposed to shots you can only hope to hit. For each hole, you should have a plan based on shots that you have at least a 50 percent chance for success with.
- *Commit yourself to target golf.* Good course management is a matter of *targets and plans.* From the first swing on the first tee until the final putt on hole number eighteen, you will do nothing but define your targets and plan realistic ways to reach them. Obviously, no plan works perfectly;

that's why it's called a plan. There will almost always be shots that stray from the plan and miss the target by a substantial margin. When this happens, you play a recovery shot that permits you to get back to your game plan as soon as possible. The other option is mentally to beat yourself up for failing to execute, and that's the classic mental *Death Move*. Even on recovery shots, you are still dealing with a target and a plan—you hope a very reasonable one. Dr. Pirozzolo says to commit 100 percent to every shot, and then use 80 percent effort to execute the shot. You do not get a peak performance by overtrying. Keep something in reserve. This will help you relax and execute under pressure.

To be aware of targets throughout your round of golf—as opposed to being totally preoccupied with hitting the ball—is a big step for a golfer. It's the difference between playing golf and spending eighteen holes trying to make golf swings. Always ask yourself, "What am I trying to do?" Then proceed with your plan by employing a swing that represents 80 percent physical effort but 100 percent mental commitment. Any time a golfer of reasonable skill sets up over a shot that requires a mere half swing and almost whiffs the shot—chunking it a few feet forward or skulling it twice the intended distance, the problem was in the *plan*. His or her conscious mind put in a call for a swing that was, in most cases, either too strong or too weak. On the downswing, the unconscious mind realized the problem and hit the panic button. The original plan was aborted, and what happened then is the golf equivalent of football's broken play. As in football, a broken play in golf, or what we call a "good miss," can sometimes work out well. It's a mistake to blame the Execution Department for a major error made by the Planning Department. On your next shot, the plan may be sound, but having lost some confidence in your ability to make a swing, you may not execute it.

BASIC TIPS FOR GOOD COURSE MANAGEMENT

- *Stay Focused.* Pay attention to what must be accomplished in the present. Tune out your three-putt on the last hole (the past). Forget the tough par 5 next hole (the future). The only important shot in the entire round is the present shot, the one you have to hit next.

- *Have Confidence.* The attitude you must walk around with is one that has you believing you will successfully hit every shot as long as you stay focused. If you are playing within your capabilities, there is no reason to doubt your ability to execute the plan and reach the target.

- *Relax.* Trying to make things happen, rather than staying relaxed and *letting them happen*, is the great builder of tension. Tension usually destroys the naturalness of your golf swing. If you feel tension building, concentrate on keeping your hands and arms soft—especially at address but all throughout the swing as well. Keep the hands and arms soft, and you dramatically increase your odds of making a good swing. Perhaps the most important words in golf are *Let go* or *Let it happen*. It's okay to be nervous, even scared, at times. However, you can and you must find a way to relax your hands and arms.

- *Hit through the Window.* Any time a golfer conducts a complete analysis of the shot that must be played, there is the possibility that he or she eventually begins seeing everything that could go wrong. In a pressure situation, you may be wise to assess your situation fairly quickly, keeping most of your preshot focus on the good, smooth swing you want to make. Stand behind your ball, then pick an aiming point about ten feet ahead of the ball that is a suspended window at the height you desire. This window image will reduce your peripheral sight and help you concentrate on the swing. Now just hit the ball through the window. Even if it is not a perfect shot, the ball will likely start on line. If there were a window out in front of you on every shot, you would accelerate the club through the ball at good speed and hit many more good shots per round. Again, avoid taking too much time analyzing; avoid all thoughts of where not to hit the ball.

- *"If I Don't Hit a Good Shot—So What."* Let's face it, many golfers put far too much pressure on themselves. Trying for perfection can be dangerous. No one is perfect, and golf will always be a game of misses. Sometimes not trying is a big tension reliever. An example could be on a crucial four-foot putt. Instead of thinking. "I must hole this putt," try telling yourself, "If I don't hole this putt, so what." No one will put you in front of a firing squad. You'll be surprised how many putts you will make. Try this same strategy in any other pressure-filled shot-making situation.

NOTES ON PHYSICAL FITNESS

Fitness and physical conditioning have increased for tour players and the general golf world over the last few years for several reasons. The top players are training with experts who have proven that exercise and strength conditioning are beneficial to nearly every professional sport. Golfers, unfortunately, are the last group of athletes to accept these truths. When the general public sees that physical conditioning enhances the level of play for these top players, they come to accept that strength training must help. Science, particularly the fields of sports medicine, biomechanics, and physical therapy, have educated the public on the benefits of stretching, weight training, and aerobic exercise. Not only do these areas of fitness improve a person's enjoyment of the game, but they improve one's lifestyle as well. And finally, the world of golf instruction has come to the realization that a golfer may have certain physical limitations, such as past injuries, limited ranges of motion, muscular weaknesses, and limited flexibilities that prevent them from executing the desired swing mechanics.

Therefore, there are several important aspects to physical conditioning that apply to improving a student's game. Combined stretching and weight training improve the flexibility and range of motion for the areas trained. Golfers rely heavily on the hips, spine, shoulders, and wrists for power production and swing consistency. When these areas are limited in their range of motion, either due to lack of strength or inflexibility, a golfer's swing is certainly going to lack in power and efficiency. Stretching is a must for the average golfer, especially the senior golfer, who is losing flexibility with the aging process. By taking a few minutes to warm up before a practice session or round, a golfer is less likely to encounter injuries and will also improve the performance of the swing. Stretching after a round or practice will also lessen the likelihood of sore muscles and stiffness the following day.

Weight training is another form of exercise that adds to a person's flexibility and range of motion. There was, and may still be, a misconception that strength training bulks up a player and decreases the flexibility and range of motion for that person. Weight training actually acts to increase blood flow to the tendons and ligaments in joints as well as stretching them with weight training movements. Both add to the flexibility of a joint. Conditioning coaches plan formats of weight training where the intensity, or weight, of the exercise is light to medium and the repetitions of an exercise are limited so that an athlete promotes strength and flexibility rather than muscle mass and bulk. The program that a body builder follows is completely different from that of a competitive athlete, especially a golfer. Golfers can use free weights, machines, elastic bands, and even medicine balls to promote strength and stability. Strength conditioning can be used to improve the framework of a golfer; the legs, hips, abdominals, back, and shoulders, so that a player has a more stable base to work with. Many top players suffer from back problems due to weaknesses in these areas. The average player may find strengthening the midsection improves coordination and sequence of movement, which is vital for creating clubhead speed. Many amateurs may actually benefit more from strengthening the shoulders, forearms, and wrists since these structures are the ones directly related to controlling the club and clubface. The left arm for right-handed golfers needs to have the appropriate strength to strike the ball with a flat or bowed wrist, and then allow the forearm to rotate to complete the squaring of the face. Anatomically, women are typically weaker than men in these areas and may see immediate improvement by doing strengthening exercises.

Strength conditioning alone may not improve a person's swing, but it may act as a catalyst for swing changes. By improving strength in certain areas, a golfer may trust a change more easily or be more apt to actually perform the desired movement.

Finally, aerobic exercise is another component of physical conditioning that simply improves a golfer's stamina and endurance. For the recreational player, aerobic exercise such as running, cycling, or swimming may just be a form of keeping active and trimming the waistline. For the serious competitor, the benefits of aerobic exercise may show up more on the weekend days of a tournament where a player's ability to keep mentally focused and keep from fatiguing may allow for a top finish. Vision, mental clarity, and physical endurance are all traits that can be associated with physical well-being.

KEEPING SCORE

There is an alternative approach to scorekeeping that for some of my students has changed their entire outlook on playing a round of golf. Instead of reporting the results of each hole in strict numerical terms, this kind of scorekeeping gives the shot-by-shot record of a given round. It lists fairways hit, greens hit in regulation, bunker saves, total number of putts, etc. You can play a point game for each fairway hit and each green hit in regulation. Try to achieve a target score. This takes your mind off the score.

Improvement in these various aspects of golf is another true indication of progress, and defining your day of golf in this way also makes you a much better course manager. When golfers concentrate on these *shot-by-shot* challenges, they stop putting themselves down for the few bad shots they hit. Over a period of time, the alternative scorecards provide an excellent readout of strengths and weaknesses, which means practice time can be budgeted all the more effectively.

SUMMARY

Course management is an interesting and critically important part of your golf game. Choosing targets and devising plans for each shot is a constant mental—and emotional—challenge that truly requires self-knowledge and a shrewd judgment of talent—your own talent, that is. When you get to the point at which you are playing smart golf—doing all the little things that make the difference between shooting 100 or 88, 86 or 78, 74 or 68, losing a match or winning it—you will be enjoying this game in the best way possible.

Unfortunately, the majority of golfers never fully recognize the importance of course management. Even after reading an entire book about course management, many golfers will go out on the course and get overwhelmed by all the strategy options. For many, also, the discipline required for all the preshot details is too much to handle. For those who build up their mental technique and really learn to think their way around the golf course, the rewards include not just well-played golf but a larger understanding of themselves and the world around them.

TOP-QUALITY TEACHERS
A Checklist for Finding the Right Instructor

Golf instructors are almost unanimous in saying, "Students come in all different skill levels and interest levels, so you can't teach the same swing to everyone. That's why I would never teach a strict method or rigid positions."

While I agree that people are different and their swings naturally differ, I also believe that a good instructor has a systematic approach to teaching and is extremely consistent in what he or she espouses. All good teachers have fundamental ideas that they stick with. As I've mentioned, bad teachers dramatically change their philosophies either from year to year, month to month, week to week, or day to day!

Consistency is an important attribute in an instructor. What you want is a teacher whose grasp of the fundamentals is complete, who has a sharp eye for your swing problems, and in turn has the patience to spoon-feed you ideas and information at appropriate intervals. Most of all, you want a teacher who can tell you the things you *cannot* do as well as what you *must* do. If this sounds like a negative approach, I find it has made my instruction more definitive and less confining for the student. Even when I describe a flaw in a pupil's swing (by using the unnerving term *Death Move*), he or she need not despair. I tell my students that parameters exist, they have options, and there is leeway in terms of what will work. But, at the edge of those parameters lies Death Valley—all the off-limits swing positions from which there is virtually no escape.

A positive attitude is a must for good teaching, but negative commentary also plays its role. In fact, it can work wonders.

Making every comment positive and upbeat is, frankly, confining, eventually confusing, and counterproductive. Sometimes you'll need to hear the words *This has got to stop*.

In this age of specialization, even golf professionals are tracking in narrower skill areas and letting go of the idea that they can master every skill category in the profession. Obviously, my choice was to concentrate on teaching, but as director of golf at high-profile country clubs, my responsibilities to the membership have been demanding and varied. To make sure all these areas were covered in a completely satisfactory manner, I assembled a staff that included people with expertise in the entire operation.

One of the things you look for in a teacher is that *he or she spends a lot of time teaching*. Without a strong support team and the ability to supervise and delegate, the club professional cannot concentrate adequately on teaching. An instructor who teaches a heavy schedule of lessons usually has solid ideas and the ability to communicate them. This is not an absolute corollary, but at the very least it is one significant clue.

Having the title "golf professional" does not automatically make someone a great golf instructor any more than the title "professor" makes someone a great educator. From our days in high school and college we all know that some instructors were better than others, even though they taught from the same books and had the same opportunities. In point of fact, some professors were infinitely better than others. Here, in brief, are the additional characteristics I feel a top-quality golf instructor will display:

■   *Commitment to becoming the best.* It's easy for teachers to say they strive for teaching excellence, but when they start counting up the hours of work, the money that must be invested, and the opportunities that must be sought out, they realize the commitment becomes difficult to fulfill. Pick a teacher who is truly committed.

- *Long roster of success stories.* A teacher's best sales tool is his or her legion of satisfied students. The two very best questions: "Do this teacher's students get better?" and "Who are they?"
- *Total understanding of the complete game.* There is more to teaching golf than the full swing. A top-notch instructor must also teach putting, chipping, bunker play, course management, club fitting, and the many other little areas students want help in. This versatility comes only through tremendous effort, preparation, and training.

ABOVE

The throwing action of a baseball pitcher will help you understand the basic law of human motion that prevails in a powerful golf swing.

- *Clear understanding of the basic swing motion.* A "quality" teacher must understand the undeniable law of human motion, as well as the basic physics of the swing itself. This law refers to a certain sequence of movements that prevails in most throwing motions, such as pitching a baseball, throwing a football, or launching a javelin.

- *Multiple ways to make the point.* Command of terminology and a creative golf vocabulary are a must for the versatile teacher. A top instructor must be able to communicate to golfers who play at all levels.

- *Confidence and interest.* Your golf instructor has to care about your progress and has to convince you of your potential. If a golf professional has to force these feelings, the student will sense it immediately.

- *A good eye and good video.* I believe so firmly in the value of video I can't imagine any serious teacher not using it. I know, from having worked with many instructors, that there are some tremendous veterans who do very well without video. The answer must be that they have extremely sharp eyes for what happens in the swing and great coaching skills. I feel my own acuity for spotting flaws and noticing small increments of progress has only been enhanced by looking at so much slow-motion, stop-action videotape of the swing. At the very least, it confirms to both me and the student that my observation was correct. The top instructor makes an accurate diagnosis time after time.

- *An ability to demonstrate.* Although not mandatory, it's awfully nice to see the teacher "do it himself or herself." This demonstration of the proper technique stimulates the student and speeds the learning process.

Fine instructors in all professions don't all do things the same way. These remarks of mine are intended to put across some of the notable attributes of an effective teacher of golf. Selecting the person who can help you improve the most will take some effort, but I promise you it will be worth your research time to find that top-quality teacher who can coach you to discover all aspects of the game of golf.

THE GREAT LEARNER

Observations on How the Top Tour Pros Practice

20

Having been lucky enough to work with many top tour pros, I would like to give you some of my observations. I'll start with a story about the greatest student, learner, and practicer since Ben Hogan—Tom Kite.

At Doral, in 1992, I was working very hard with Kite on several difficult swing changes. Knowing Kite, I told him exactly what I thought about the status of his technique. That is what he always wants from me. He determined that what I told him was correct, so we set about making the changes on Tuesday of tournament week.

Now, understand that when Kite works on something he puts 100 percent effort into it. We made a dramatic change in his follow-through, which was geared to altering his swing path through impact. We taped it, reviewed it, retaped, reviewed again, and again, and again. This despite the fact that Doral tour event began in just two days.

All too soon, it was Thursday, tournament time. One of my instructors followed Kite on the first three holes that morning and it wasn't pretty. He came back and told me that Tom had hit the worst snap hook ever on hole number three into a lake about 150 yards off the tee—and this came after a five, five start. Needless to say, my heart sank. Could I have ruined Kite? Was he on his way to his highest score of the year?

About four hours later Kite walked onto the tee at the Doral Learning Center, and I went over to meet him. Not knowing what he shot, I simply asked him (with my heart in my throat).

QUALITY STUDENTS . . .

1. Listen intently.
2. Clarify problems.
3. Ask questions.
4. Don't expect immediate results.
5. Persevere.
6. Are determined to succeed.
7. Trust the teacher.
8. Don't complain about minor setbacks.
9. Follow the game plan devised with their teacher.
10. Write down swing "thoughts" and "feels."
11. Set reachable goals within a set time frame.
12. Don't always judge their progress by ball flight.

Thankfully, it was seventy-three. Next, I asked him how he hit the ball. Kite said he had started weak but had hit some excellent shots. I then said, "I heard about the drive on number three—did you just forget about what we were working on after that and get back to something you could play with to get it around for today?"

I was a little taken back by Kite's response, which was, "What do you mean, Jim?"

So I had to start over. "Well, did you go back to some different ideas?"

Tom looked at me as if I were crazy. He said forcefully, "Jim, I made a few bad swings out there, but the thought of changing never occurred to me. I *know* we are working on the right things. I don't care how I hit it today—I'm going to make the corrections necessary for the future."

That was the end of the conversation. We went right back to working on *the same things*.

Incidentally, on Sunday, the last round, Tom hit every fairway with his driver and all eighteen greens in regulation. He came down to the Learning Center all pumped up and told me it was the best ball-striking round he had experienced in more than a year. He finished 66, 69 on the weekend, for a sixth-place finish. One month later he won at Atlanta and soon after captured the U.S. Open at Pebble Beach.

More recently, I have been struck by the work ethic of Tiger Woods. Most everybody assumes he is just supertalented; however, a great part of his success is due to his desire to be great. Tiger really does work harder than anyone else on the PGA Tour. All those victories are directly related to his incredible work ethic. Far from taking a soft approach, Tiger relentlessly pursues greatness.

Tiger's swing coach, Butch Harmon, is a great friend of mine. We have worked together often and his teaching style has many similarities to mine. Both of us depart from concepts that eliminate lateral motion or initiating the swing in some newfangled theory. We are much more fundamental in our approaches, knowing there is no magic teaching lesson, only practice.

Teaching golf is a "moving target" with every student. Golf is game of upgrading and change. Somedays we just don't have it or don't quite feel it the same way. I mention this because I believe Tiger Woods understands this perfectly. He trusts Butch and does not blame the coach when he has an off week. Instead he goes right back to work on the fundamentals.

It should reassure all of us that even Tiger Woods still takes lessons and does occasionally have a bad game. What is important to realize is that Woods always keeps his enthusiasm and his spirit. He is not about to give up or get down for too long. Instead you'll find him out on the range or practicing his swing in front of a mirror. Despite being the number one player in the world, Woods still gets excited about hitting a perfect shot, and his enthusiasm for the game only grows.

The thought occurred to me: Here is the number one player in the world as excited about a great practice-range drive as any young teenager might be smoking a long, straight tee shot. Maybe more excited!

There is a big lesson here. *Appreciate the brilliant shots you hit. Give yourself credit. Remember your good shots and make them important—even on the practice tee.*

Most golfers do just the opposite. They make a big deal about the bad shots, throwing clubs or criticizing themselves unmercifully. Don't. Take a lesson from the world's greatest students.

Woods and Kite play golf because they love it. To them it is *art*. They paint pictures with their clubs. Neither one can wait for the next day of golf.

Great students love the game.

SHORT TIPS

Short but Great Tips on the Golf Swing

1. The golf swing moves in a circle—as viewed from *overhead!!*

2. The big muscles of your body provide the extra power to accelerate the arms and club.

3. Your arms guide the club on the plane:

    - they respond to the motions of the body
    - they *do not* function independently of the pivot motions

4. Your hands are a primary source of information to the brain about what the clubhead and clubface are doing. The eyes are equally important.

    - the hands are used to fine-tune the shot
    - it can be useful to think of the back of the left hand as having the same alignment as the clubface

5. A proper pivot (body motion) is critical to a great golf swing.

6. Based upon the amount of time you practice properly, major changes may take six months to a year.

7. You retain very little (5 percent) of what you hear. Most people learn much better through:

    - demonstrations
    - pictures

- training aids
- drills
- feeling the change

8. If you are nonathletic you can become a good player, but you will require more attention, supervision, perseverance, and dedicated practice.

9. *Master the basics* is a great learning concept. Make sure you are a master of:

- setup
- alignments
- grip pressure
- balance, tempo, rhythm
- the finish

10. Mirrors are great coaches.

11. Most golfers should and are capable of getting better, the problem is they don't.

12. *Nothing* is correct for everyone. Every tip I have ever heard or read is correct for somebody at sometime. Most tips you hear will not pertain to your swing.

13. To improve your golf swing, do the following:

- make a commitment to do what is necessary
- be willing to change
- schedule time to practice
- be realistic about how hard and long it takes for lasting improvement
- believe in what you are doing

14. "Practice" does not necessarily mean standing on the range banging balls hour after hour.

15.   Proper use of your range time is an important part of improving. Make sure you are making the correct practice moves.

16.   There are many things that can be improved upon and learned that *do not* require you to go to the range.

17.   Change your target from time to time when at the range.

18.   Do not practice longer than you can stay focused. If you can't concentrate, *quit.*

19.   Rhythm, Timing, and Balance are as important as swing mechanics.

20.   Talent is God-given, technique can be learned.

21.   Demanding that golf instruction be simple is a fallacy. The golf swing is a series of moves that is in fact not simple for most people. Incomplete instruction can take you only so far and then it becomes ineffective. What a good teacher can often do is make very simple points that are also very clear to the student. That is great teaching. However, this same teacher will continue to build a better swing piece by piece, a little at a time, simple point by simple point. This building block approach is how almost anyone can build a highly effective golf swing.

22.   A careless beginning can be disastrous.

23.   A good golfer plans for success.

24.   Tension kills the golf swing!!

25.   Most shots are missed at setup.

26.   *Enthusiasm without truth* equals "frustration" (Dave Collins, Jim McLean Master Instructor).

MASTERY
Learning the Eight-Step Swing

Mention the word *practice* and most golfers picture driving ranges, blistered hands, sore muscles, and in recognition of this suffering, a small dose of success. No teaching professional, least of all this one, will deny the value of practicing correctly on the driving range. But hitting balls at the range is only part of the answer. Former Masters winner Claude Harmon figured this out long ago and would lament often about frustrated golfers trying to improve by mindlessly "beating balls" on the range.

Claude would tell a story about a man who buys a new $200,000 Ferrari, jumps in his car, then leaves Winged Foot Golf Club (in Westchester County, New York, where Claude taught) headed for New York City. He's on I-95, but mistakenly heads north instead of south. He puts the pedal to the floorboard and races down the highway at top speed, 180 miles per hour. He's making great time, but he's got two serious problems: he's getting farther from New York City with every mile, and he's liable to kill himself in the process. Like the golfer beating balls with no clue, Claude would say, the man in the Ferrari has no direction, and sadly he will never reach his destination.

For some, too much practice on the range may actually impede progress. I have spent half my life on the practice range, and I promise you, there are more than a few golfers who hit balls on the range hour upon hour, day after day, and gain little if any benefit from their efforts. "More is better" does not always apply to practicing golf. The secret is to devote your time, whether it's a minute or several hours, to *practical practice*.

Correct golf movements might begin in the intellect, but they must end in the muscles, and muscle memory is cultivated through practice. People with superior physical aptitude will learn faster, but there is no one who becomes an excellent golfer without paying the price on "the rock pile." For a fundamental change to occur in your swing, there must be sufficient time for the conscious and unconscious mind to accept it. My rule of thumb is to allow about one month of steady effort for the student to internalize one significant component of a swing change. Then he or she can go on to the next new move.

The player who works consistently on solid fundamentals and makes progress in small segments will tend not to lose overnight what he or she has gained over time. When the player does slide backward, the slide will be minor and the turnaround not long in the making. There are no shortcuts to the mastery of golf; intelligent practice is the only way to narrow the gap between knowing something about the swing and employing it correctly.

I like to believe I have helped some players simply by changing their entire outlook on practice. Practice doesn't have to be just hitting balls down a driving range. It can be fun. It can be in short sessions. It can take place at home or in your backyard, and it can be greatly enhanced if you adopt a positive attitude toward the game and read helpful books and articles and study videotapes.

One interesting example along these lines occurred with Gary Player at my former Learning Center at Sleepy Hollow. During a practice session, I brought Gary inside to watch some particular video footage of Ben Hogan. It is some awesome footage of two specific swings that I knew Gary would love to see. Sure enough, he was tremendously interested. I replayed each swing hundreds of times, and we viewed the tape for more than two hours. Gary spent a great deal of time talking about what he saw and knew about Hogan.

After this in-depth viewing, Gary went back to the practice tee with more enthusiasm and a vivid picture of what he wanted to do. The next day he shot 66 in our senior tour event. Full credit went to those beautiful pictures of Hogan that stayed clearly in Gary's mind. I know, because he told me that the tape gave him a completely new feel and picture of what he was trying to do.

You are practicing whenever you are repeating exercises and drills on a regular basis, no matter where you happen to be. Golfers who are retooling their full swings often wonder if they can improve by taking one or two lessons or whether they need a six-or eight-week series. The number of formal lessons you take can be reduced significantly if you and your instructor can devise a detailed, comprehensive practice program that, incidentally, *will* involve doing swing drills without hitting balls.

Practice the Eight-Step Swing using a regular club, swing fan, or a weighted club. It is very helpful to swing in front of a mirror, and I know this will work for you if you are diligent. Put yourself in the correct positions (the positions you need to improve) and hold each one—over and over, the more repetitions the better. The more you practice in this way, the quicker your old habits and your old swing problems will melt away. Realize that changing a physical habit requires constant attention and repetition. I know one thing for sure; everyone is different. Some will change quickly; others will take much more time.

When you are on the range hitting balls, always execute a significant number of your shots using your full preshot routine. At least 20 percent of your shots on the range should be hit following a full implementation of your preshot pattern. This is practicing as you would play. It adds a whole dimension to practice. Try to hit two of every ten shots using a target and a preshot routine. This way, your practice will at least somewhat *simulate* actual play.

To enjoy golf to the fullest, you have to learn to enjoy the journey, with all its peaks and valleys and its occasional long plateaus. Reaching the final lofty destination takes a long time and focused attention on practicing the correct movements. It is not the destination, however, that is always most important.

ABOVE

Practicing with a weighted "donut" on your club helps you groove a good swing. Here holding the correct delivery position.

Instead, it is the striving and the paths you choose that provide the fun of golf. On some lucky days, you'll even feel that you are zipping along in a new Ferrari—headed in the absolutely correct direction, too.

GOOD AND BAD PRACTICE SWINGS

Ever heard someone say, "My practice swing is great, but when I go to hit the ball my swing is terrible"? We've all heard that statement groaned a thousand times. Has it ever struck you as somewhat illogical? If not, it should.

It isn't so much that the person's swing at the ball is so poor as that the practice swing is far less good than he or she thinks it is. Usually the poor golfer has far overrated his or her practice swing. Most people have the same body movements and swing mistakes in their practice swing as in their real swing. What changes is their *tempo* and the fact that they are not impacting an object. Because they swing slowly with no fear of mishitting the ball, their practice swing feels pretty good. Only it isn't. The same mistakes that plague the real swing are there in the practice swing all along.

Practice swings are like push-ups. One push-up does nothing—but hundreds of push-ups done on a regular basis have a dramatic effect. Your practice swings are governed by a similar dynamic of repetition. Done correctly, the practice swing will eventually produce dramatic improvements. Done haphazardly—perhaps instilling Death Moves—the practice swing will only make improvement that much more elusive.

THE VALUE OF PRACTICE SWINGS AND DRILLS

I teach students from every walk and way of life. Golf has a varying degree of importance to each. There is no way for me, or any other instructor, to come up with a single practice schedule that will fit all golfers. There are too many variables. One breakthrough I have experienced with a broad range of students is to get them to appreciate the value of swinging the club or working on body motions. I encourage them to take practice swings at home, in the office, or in any setting where they can find just a few minutes. Getting them to make practice swings from a proper set to a proper follow-through for brief sessions has brought about significant swing improvements for many. Consistent, short practice sessions are usually much more beneficial than sporadic long sessions. This focused consistent approach speeds improvement. Significantly!

Equally important is the use of drills. Athletes in all sports work on drills to perfect their body actions and tune their muscles. Golf had lagged far behind other sports in this regard. To get better faster, by all means use appropriate drills. They will speed your improvement.

Whenever I teach a particular position of the Eight-Step Swing, I find that drills are highly effective. Students quickly learn what to feel and look for when correctly executing each position, and they learn how to arrive at each position. Students also understand that for each position there is an acceptable variance. In other words, there is usually room for a different look. This point is vital. When changing a position in your swing, it's extremely helpful to view your swing constantly in a mirror (or watch it on videotape); it is important that you learn how to look at a golf swing and why good swings don't all look the same. The main reason they look different is that body size, physique, rhythm, tempo, and backswing locations differ so markedly from player to player. Picture the swings of these golfers: Miller Barber, Curtis Strange, Ben Hogan, Jack Nicklaus, David Frost, Nick Price, Jeff Sluman, and Nancy Lopez. Obviously, they are not carbon copies of each other, despite the fact that in their own ways, each player achieves the basic fundamental positions.

Now picture these players facing you in a police lineup. Considering how different they are in basic physique (not to mention the differences in metabolism, muscle tissue, and other internal systems), is it any surprise that their golf swings don't look alike on the surface? It should not be a surprise at all. The more you learn what to look for, however, the more the *similarities* will appear to you.

HOW TO KNOW YOU ARE MAKING PROGRESS

Can you do it? Can you make a significant swing change or swing adjustment? The answer depends on your determination more than any other factor, but I believe it will be yes. By working with a qualified PGA teaching professional who will help keep you motivated and spot mistakes, most golfers can achieve their own acceptable version of the efficient, powerful golf swing shown in the Eight Steps. You'll know you are within reach of a consistent, fundamentally correct swing action when you can automatically go through the step or steps you have changed with no mechanical thought. Again, to achieve dramatic results or to make a significant swing change, practice must be a constant, everyday activity. Even devoting a few minutes a day to practical practice will make a tremendous difference.

THE "FEEL" SIDE: TIMING AND BALANCE

Like all physical gifts, natural balance and fluid rhythm are not parceled out evenly to everyone. Yet they are probably the most important attributes of the athlete. Some players will never achieve that wonderful, graceful ease of motion that has made Sam Snead, Al Geiberger, Bruce Lietzke, Fred Couples, Phil Mickelson, Anika Sorenstam, Meg Mallon, and Carrie Webb so fun to watch. But you can still work toward improving your rhythm and balance. Physical conditioning and flexibility are factors in the achievement of fluid, even-tempo motion.

To improve your balance, rhythm, and tempo further, you should watch and imitate athletes who embody it. Whenever you can watch a top tour player, make sure to do so with an eye toward recording his or her tempo and storing the "tape" in some corner of your mind. When you get back home, let your body sense that same rhythm. This is the best way to smooth out your swing and keep it from being rigid, nonathletic, and mechanical. Sometimes imitation—the old monkey-see, monkey-do—is the best way to learn. When you practice your swing, work hard on the coordination of your body parts. Focus on timing the club, arms, and body evenly. Sense a balance of all your parts and simplify your motion by using a 1–2–3–4 count or repeating a tune inside your head.

CONCLUDING REMARKS

In this book I have detailed the system I use to teach the golf swing. The information contained within serves as a major portion of what my instructors must know to teach at our schools. That of course means this is an "in-depth study."

I want to mention one more time, as I conclude this work, that we do not teach eight individual steps to our students. Many times I will not even mention the word *step*. Rather it is a precision diagnostic tool that breaks down the swing into key checkpoints. When you at least *basically understand* where your swing should be at specific locations, you too can accurately diagnose your own golf swing. With this book you have the tools to dissect the inner workings and components of a powerful and accurate swing action.

To me, steps make the swing understandable. When I first broke the golf swing into body action and club action and combined it with the "Corridors of Success," I knew I was onto an entirely new way of helping my students. The bottom line is that the system works. We prove it every day at all of our schools and we have been doing it for a long time.

When you get right down to it, great teaching is simply the

ability to help people improve. A top teacher can do it time after time with any type of student. That's what I call "total game instruction," and improving the full golf swing is probably the most fun aspect of it all. With the Eight-Step System I've seen a wide range of instructors have tremendous success with all types of students. I'm also very confident this system will work for you.

I wish you all the best of luck with your golf. Remember to enjoy the process. Remember to break the golf swing down to an action you can master. Then build on that success. The "building block approach" works the best in every sport and in every learning process I have ever studied. The golf swing is complex, but we need to make it understandable and as simple as we possibly can. The only way I know to do this is by learning, understanding, and then executing the fundamentals and the basic moves that golf demands.

Enjoy the journey.